FROM FAIRY TALES
Alice in Wonderland

Karen in the Red Shoes

INSTRUCTIONS ON PAGE 72

Red-Riding Hood

3

MARY

CARRIE

the Big Woods

LAURA

JO

BETH

Women

MEG

AMY

INSTRUCTIONS ON PAGE 80

Monday's child is fair of face,
Tuesday's child is full of grace,
Wednesday's child is full of woe,
Thursday's child has far to go,
Friday's child is loving and giving,
Saturday's child works hard for a living,
But the child that is born on the Sabbath day
is bonny and blithe, and good and gay.

Monday's child

Tuesday's child

Wednesday's child

Thursday's child   Friday's child   Saturday's child   Sunday's child

The Sound of Music
MARIA

My Fair Lady
ELIZA

HUG-DOLLS

·Rosalie·

INSTRUCTIONS ON PAGE 93

Ellen

INSTRUCTIONS ON PAGE 94

◖ INSTRUCTIONS ON PAGE 97
◑ INSTRUCTIONS ON PAGE 98

Shigeru & Chiko

Midori & Oyuki

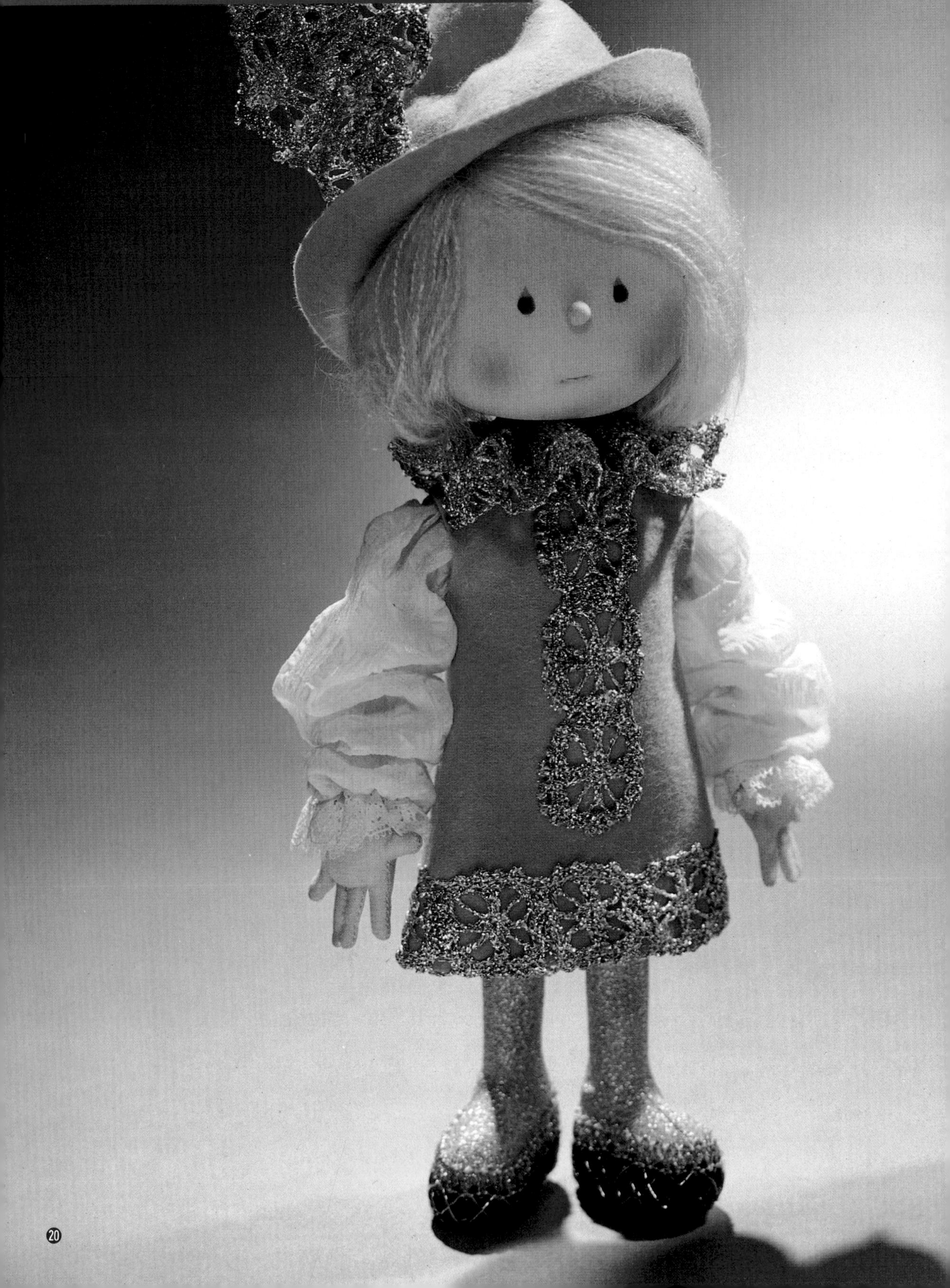

Prince of the Moon
&
Princess of the Flowers

The Wood Elves

INSTRUCTIONS ON PAGE 109

Lost Angels

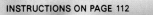

INSTRUCTIONS ON PAGE 112

The Land of Unborn Babies

INSTRUCTIONS ON PAGE 113

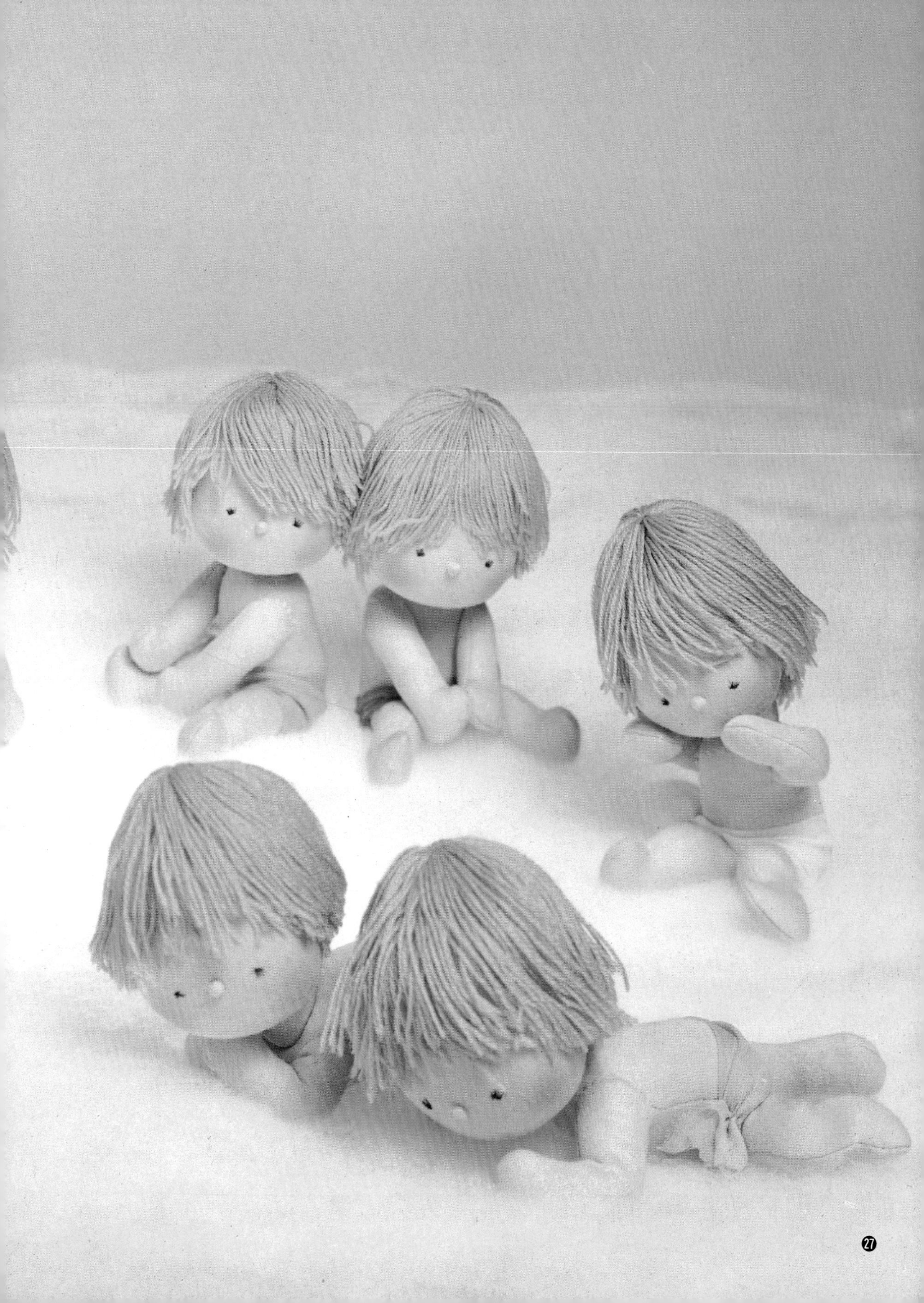

Nymph Ondeena

INSTRUCTIONS ON PAGE 114

Puck, Who Works for the King of Spirits

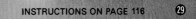

INSTRUCTIONS ON PAGE 116

Pippi
Longstocking

INSTRUCTIONS ON PAGE 118

Willful Lotta

INSTRUCTIONS ON PAGE 121

INSTRUCTIONS ON PAGE 130 **37**

Rapunzel
with Golden Hair

INSTRUCTIONS ON PAGE 131

Princess Elissa
in the Moon Light

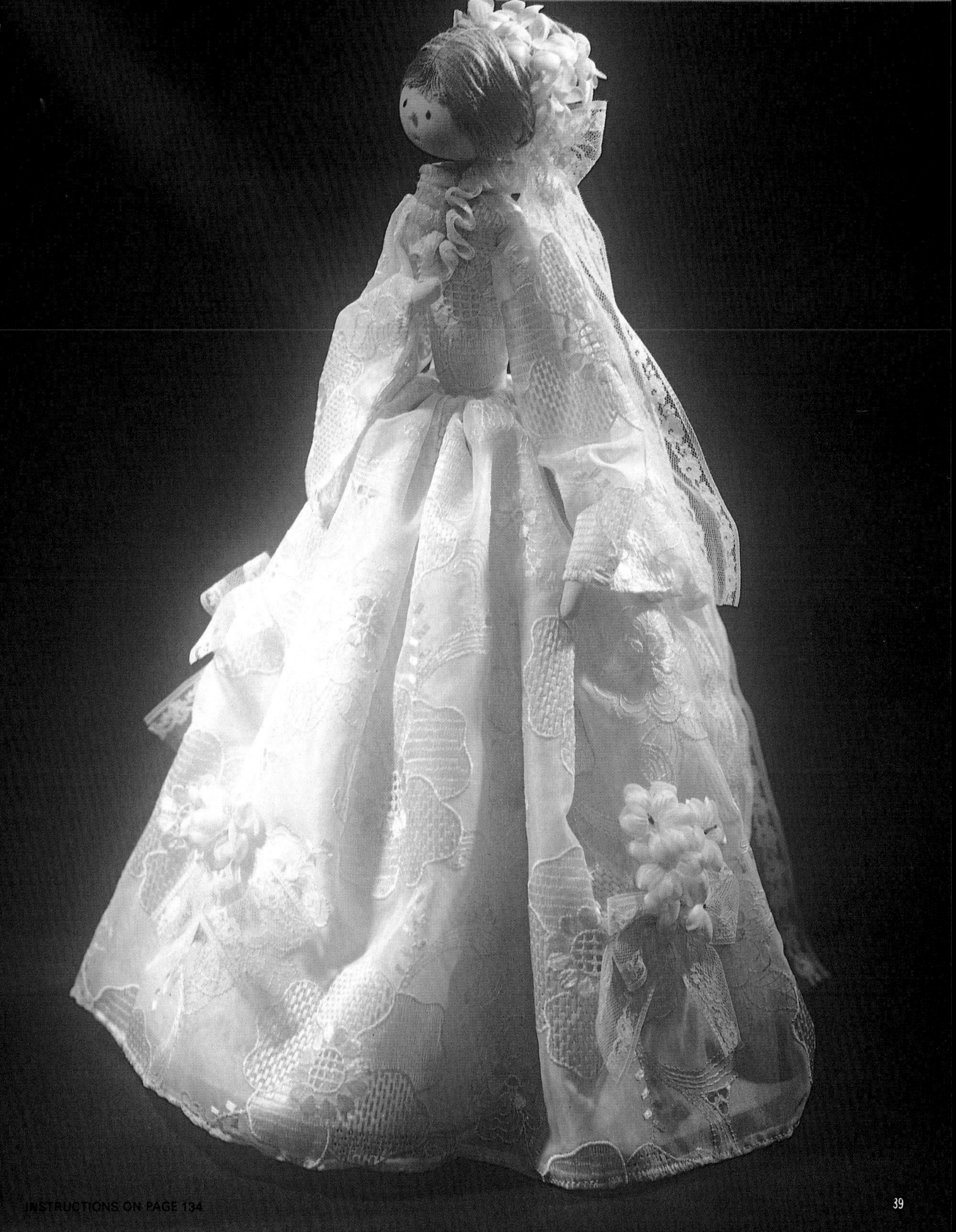

INSTRUCTIONS ON PAGE 134

Royal Princess
of the Stars

INSTRUCTIONS ON PAGE 136

Madam Lilac
in Her Own Color

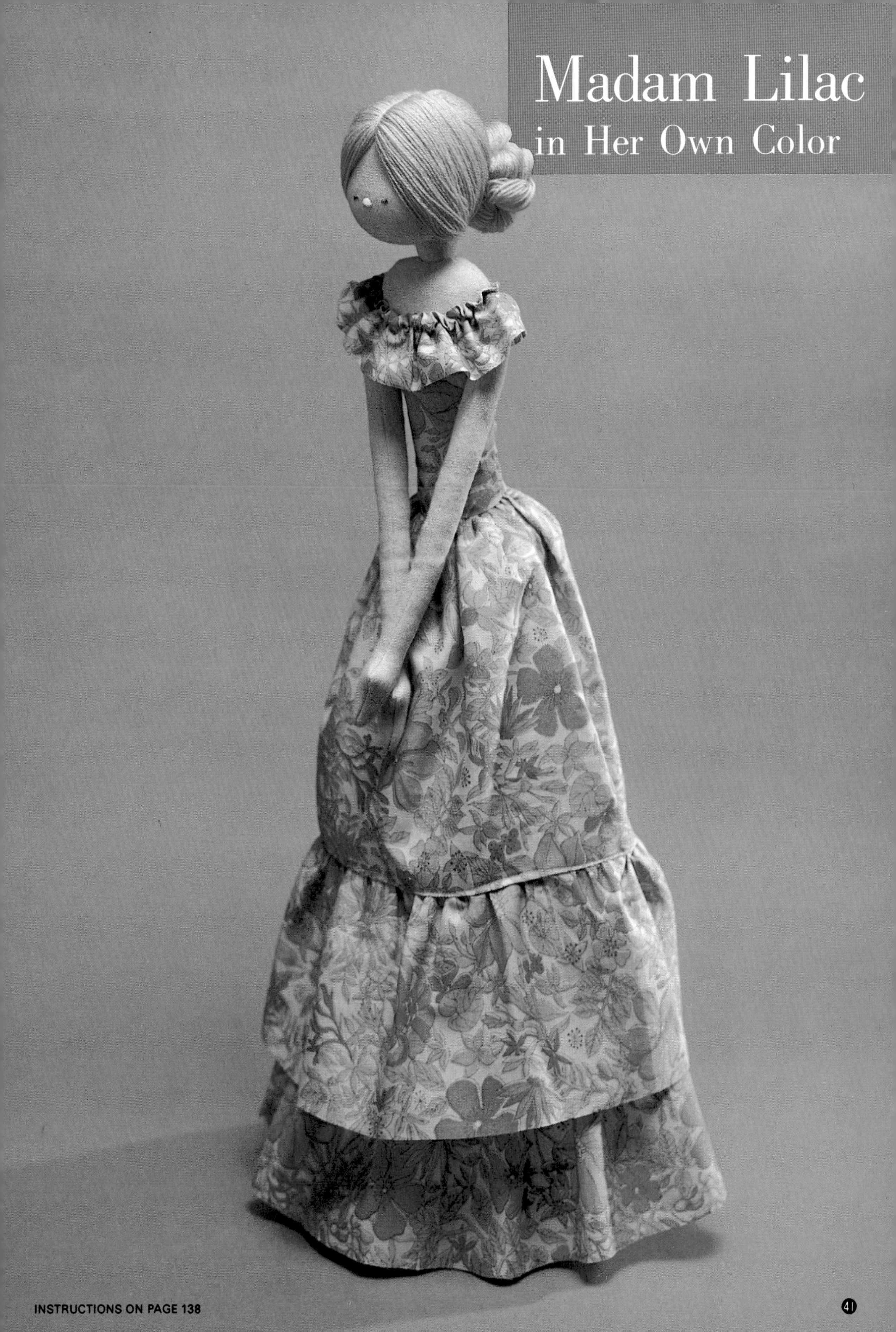

INSTRUCTIONS ON PAGE 138

John & Barbara

INSTRUCTIONS ON PAGE 140

Mimi & Lulu & Popo

かぐや姫

Princess from the Land of Bamboo

INSTRUCTIONS ON PAGE 143

GENERAL INFORMATION FOR STUFFED DOLLS

LET'S MAKE "HIJI"

Hiji is an engaging hug-doll with a large oval head. Step-by-step directions for making her are shown on the following pages, and it's a good way for beginners to practice new skills.

You'll find that the secret of making a good doll is its foundation. Heads can be made larger or smaller, as you wish, but proper stuffing gives the doll a finished look. You can later vary their appearance by the shape and color of hair and clothing, and you'll find these projects are a good use for scraps in your sewing basket.

Welcome to the new pleasures of doll-making, then. You'll be creating thoughtful and personalized keepsakes in no time!

HIJI FINISHED SIZE: 37 cm tall

HOW TO MAKE "HIJI"

★ MATERIALS:

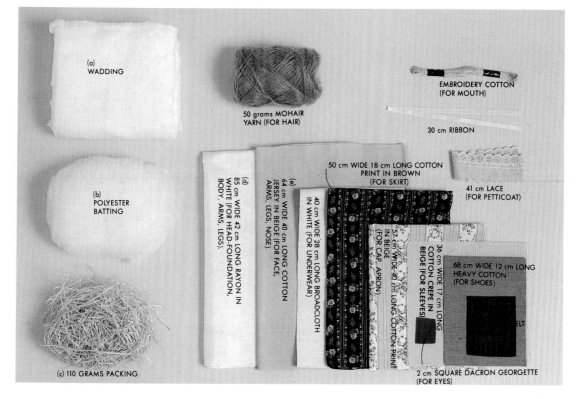

(a) WADDING

50 grams MOHAIR YARN (FOR HAIR)

EMBROIDERY COTTON (FOR MOUTH)

30 cm RIBBON

(b) POLYESTER BATTING

(d) 85 cm WIDE 42 cm LONG RAYON IN WHITE (FOR HEAD-FOUNDATION, BODY, ARMS, LEGS).

(e) 64 cm WIDE 40 cm LONG COTTON JERSEY IN BEIGE (FOR FACE, ARMS, LEGS, NOSE).

40 cm WIDE 28 cm LONG BROADCLOTH IN WHITE (FOR UNDERWEAR)

57 cm WIDE 40 cm LONG COTTON PRINT

50 cm WIDE 18 cm LONG COTTON PRINT IN BROWN (FOR SKIRT)

41 cm LACE (FOR PETTICOAT)

IN BEIGE (FOR CAP, APRON).

36 cm WIDE 17 cm LONG COTTON CREPE IN BEIGE (FOR SLEEVES)

68 cm WIDE 12 cm LONG HEAVY COTTON (FOR SHOES)

FELT

(c) 110 GRAMS PACKING

2 cm SQUARE DACRON GEORGETTE (FOR EYES)

(a) to (e) are the materials needed to make the foundation; (a) to (c) are stuffing materials to form the foundation. Have extra amounts of stuffing material on hand. Other materials, such as yarn or cotton fabrics, can be selected from remnants you way have.

Assemble machine threads No. 50, 20, 8, and hand-sewing thread. When you make the foundation, use white thread with the long, heavy needle.

★ TOOLS:

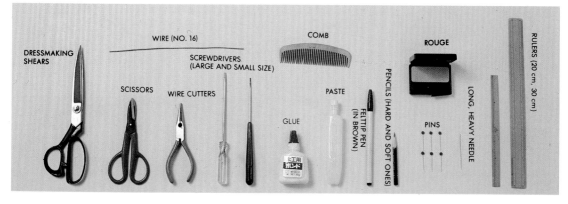

DRESSMAKING SHEARS

WIRE (NO. 16)

SCREWDRIVERS (LARGE AND SMALL SIZE)

COMB

ROUGE

RULERS (20 cm, 30 cm)

SCISSORS

WIRE CUTTERS

PASTE

PENCILS (HARD AND SOFT ONES)

LONG, HEAVY NEEDLE

GLUE

FELTTIP PEN (IN BROWN)

PINS

1 TO MAKE PATTERNS:

Make cardboard patterns for accuracy. Copy each of the patterns below on tracing paper, and then transfer onto cardboard, making the outline with a hard pencil. Cut out the cardboard patterns carefully. Transfer the arrows, too, to show the grain of fabric for cutting.

GUIDE LINES BELOW:

————— =FINISHED OUTLINE

—·—·— = OPENING FOR STUFFING

— — — = FOLD LINE

←——→ =LENGTHWISE GRAIN OF FABRIC

PATTERNS (ACTUAL SIZE):

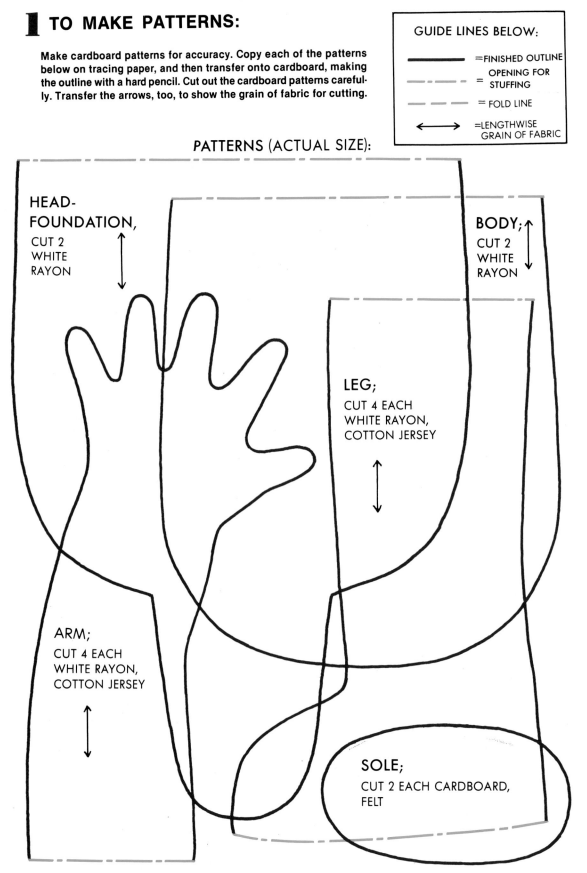

HEAD-FOUNDATION,
CUT 2
WHITE
RAYON

BODY;
CUT 2
WHITE
RAYON

LEG;
CUT 4 EACH
WHITE RAYON,
COTTON JERSEY

ARM;
CUT 4 EACH
WHITE RAYON,
COTTON JERSEY

SOLE;
CUT 2 EACH CARDBOARD,
FELT

52

2 TO SEW HEAD-FOUNDATION, BODY, ARMS & LEGS:

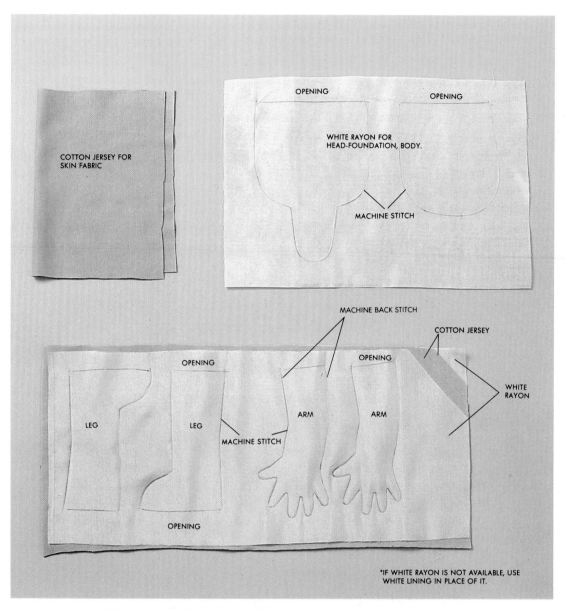

COTTON JERSEY FOR SKIN FABRIC

OPENING   OPENING

WHITE RAYON FOR HEAD-FOUNDATION, BODY.

MACHINE STITCH

MACHINE BACK STITCH

COTTON JERSEY

WHITE RAYON

OPENING   OPENING

LEG   LEG   ARM   ARM

MACHINE STITCH

OPENING

*IF WHITE RAYON IS NOT AVAILABLE, USE WHITE LINING IN PLACE OF IT.

Iron fabrics smooth. Trace the head-foundation onto white rayon, matching grain to arrows, and machine stitch.

Place the skin-colored jersey, right sides together, between 2 pieces of white rayon; then trace on the patterns for 2 arms and legs.

Machine stitch along traced lines, leaving an opening for stuffing.

Cut out the pieces, leaving the following seam allowances: 1.5 cm at openings of arms and legs, 0.6 cm around fingers, 0.2 cm on curved areas of fingers; and 1.5 cm around all the head-foundation areas of the body.

3 TO MAKE A HEAD-FOUNDATION & BODY:

Turn white rayon foundation pieces right-side out and stuff firmly with packing material, using a screw driver. If more packing is needed, adding it before completely stuffing in the first amount will give a smooth, firm finish.

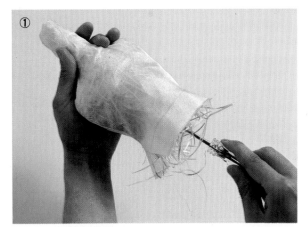
①

① Finish the neck of the head-foundation as firm as a bar, stuffing to right above the opening line.

② Sew along opening, turn allowance to wrong side and draw stitches to close end firmly. Secure again, working a crossed stitch over it.

③ Stuff packing firmly into the body up to the opening. Lap the ends, matching opening lines together and pin it steady.

④ Secure firmly with 2 strands of No. 8 machine thread, making rough stitches.

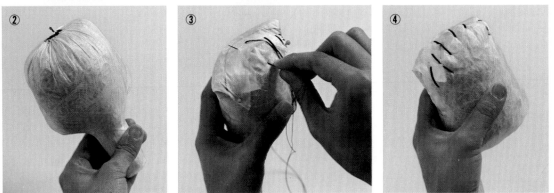
② ③ ④

4 TO FORM THE BASE OF FACE:

Form the cotton wadding by tearing off the pieces needed with your hand. Head-foundation, jaw, and forehead are arranged as follows.

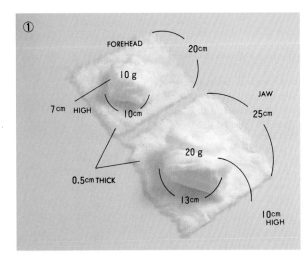
①
FOREHEAD   20cm
10 g
7cm HIGH   10cm
JAW
25cm
0.5cm THICK
20 g
13cm
10cm HIGH

②

① Make jaw first, and then forehead.

② Roll the piece up firmly, putting wadding piece for padding inside.

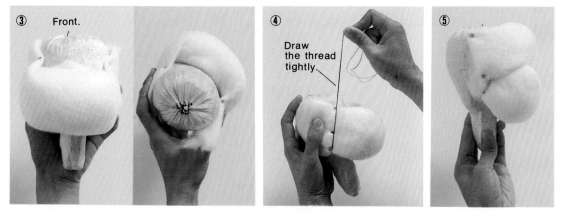

③ Front.

④ Draw the thread tightly.

⑤

③ Attach jaw piece to the head-foundation with the jaw facing slightly downward, then make it steady with pins.

④ Sew on head-foundation with No. 8 machine thread doubled, drawing large stitches. Tear away surplus wadding on the sides.

⑤ Attach forehead. Pin the piece steady, drawing lower ends on both sides slightly over the jaw piece. Tear away the surplus wadding and tuck in all ends.

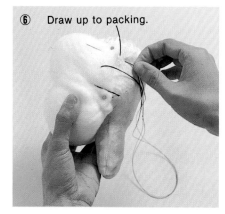

⑥ Draw up to packing.

⑦ Leave no space between.

LEAVE NO SPACE BETWEEN

⑧

⑥ Stitch the ends at the side firmly to head-foundation.

⑦ Front

⑧ Back side

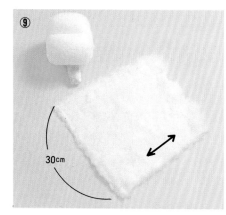

⑨

30cm

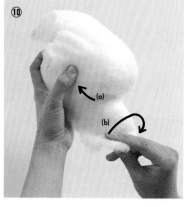

⑩

(a)

(b)

⑪

⑨ Spread wadding piece of 0.5 cm thickness. Lay on face at the bias.

⑩ Pull wadding upward, fitting to the shape of jaw (a). Wrap lower part round the neck as (b).

⑪ Smooth surface, fitting overlaid wadding carefully to the base. Tear away surplus at the back.

5 TO COVER THE BASE OF FACE WITH SKIN FABRIC:

Because of the elasticity of cotton jersey as a skin fabric, pin the ends of the stretched piece firmly to the base so the fabric does not become loose.

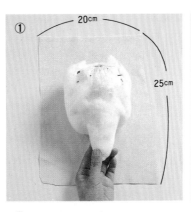

① Place face side down in the middle of skin fabric.

② Pin (a) to steady. Pull up the ends, both sides at a time, shoping the jaw. Pin (b) to the base so the fabric does not become loose.

③ Twist top corners, be careful not to make any folds on forehead; cross them on back and pin to hold steady (c).

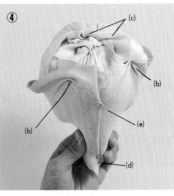

④ Fold back the surplus at back neck, and pin to hold steady (d) (e).

⑤ Stitch to the head-foundation with No. 8 machine thread doubled, pulling the fabric slightly upward.

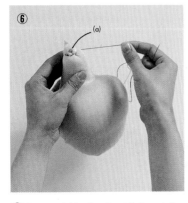

⑥ Secure (a) to the foundation, taking 3-4 stitches with single strand of No. 8 machine thread.

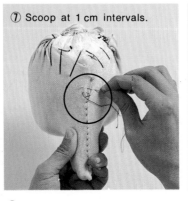

⑦ With No. 8 thread, work fine stitches taking care not to make the fabric loosen at center back.

⑦ Scoop at 1 cm intervals.

⑧ Finished foundation.

6 TO ATTACH EYES, NOSE & MOUTH:

Experiment by placing eyes, nose, and mouth on face until you have the expression you want; then mark their position lightly on the face with a pencil.

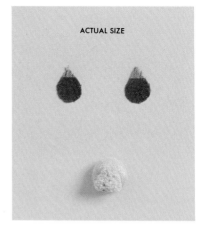

ACTUAL SIZE

TO MAKE A NOSE

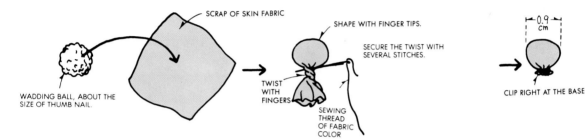

SCRAP OF SKIN FABRIC

SHAPE WITH FINGER TIPS.

SECURE THE TWIST WITH SEVERAL STITCHES.

WADDING BALL, ABOUT THE SIZE OF THUMB NAIL.

TWIST WITH FINGERS

SEWING THREAD OF FABRIC COLOR

0.9 cm

CLIP RIGHT AT THE BASE

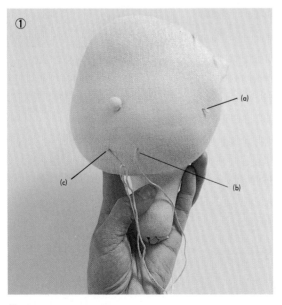

① Glue nose in position.
Use strands of cotton to make a mouth. Carry the needle through following (a) (b) (c) in turn, bring the needle out opposite (a), fasten off the thread, pulling sligthly.

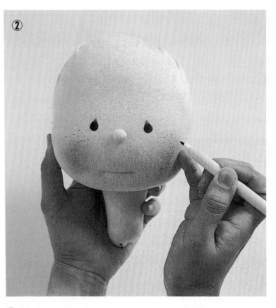

② Make eyes of dacron georgette. Pulling out upper crosswise threads to make eyelashes. Cut into shape and glue in place.
Apply rouge using wadding piece. Make freckles lightly with felttip pen. The ink might spread on the fabric, so try on another scrap first.

7 TO MAKE ARMS:

Make plump hands, stuffing wadding into fingers and polyester batting into arms.

① Cut out arms with seam allowances, clip at the curve.

② Turn inside out using screw driver.

③ Turn fingers right side out one by one.

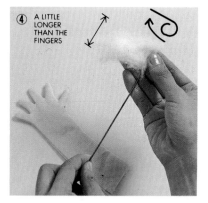

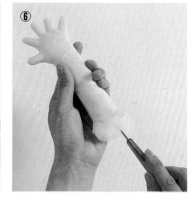

④ Wrap a piece of wadding round the No. 16 wire.

⑤ Insert into each finger and pull out the wire, leaving wadding piece inside.

⑥ Stuff polyester batting into arm using screw driver. Put a little piece into palm side, making back side of the hand plump. Hand-stitch along opening, turning allowances inside, then fasten off.

8 TO MAKE LEGS:

Make legs, stuffing cotton wadding firmly.

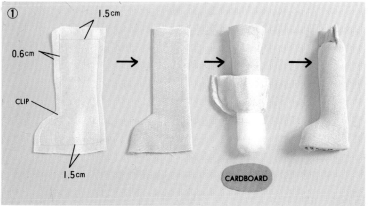

① Clip at the curve, then turn inside out.

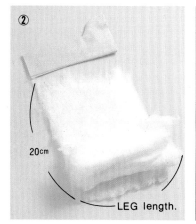

② Put wadding for padding on the stretched wadding piece.

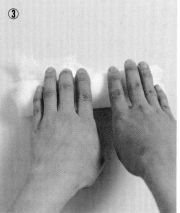

③ Roll together firmly into leg size.

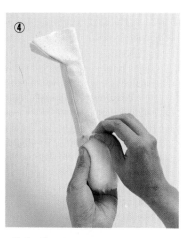

④ Stuff rolled wadding into the top opening.

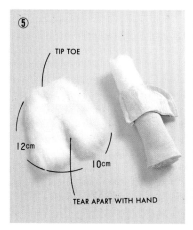

⑤ Make a piece of wadding for foot.

⑥ Put lower end of the leg between the tear, wrap with the next piece.

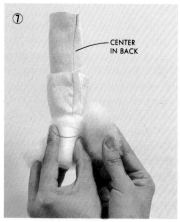

⑦ Lap surplus wadding at back, pull down the foot fabric above. Stitch top opening closed and fasten off.

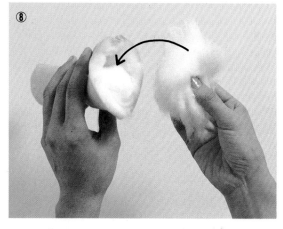

⑧ Stuff wadding up to the line of the sole.

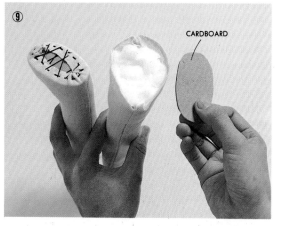

⑨ Insert the cardboard sole. Hand-stitch along the sole and draw the thread, overcasting a few times crosswise, then secure the end.

❾ TO PUT ON SHOES:

Cut out the pieces of shoes from fabric, referring to page 62. Make with glue.

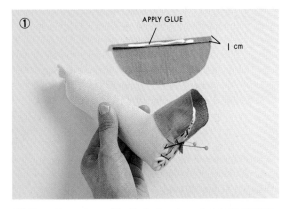

① Turn the edge of half-circle piece 1 cm to wrong side, apply glue on it. Pin it to foot, covering instep.

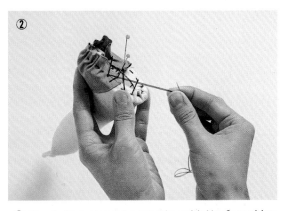

② Hand-stitch along the cut edge with No. 8 machine thread doubled, draw the thread overcasting a few times crosswise, secure the end.

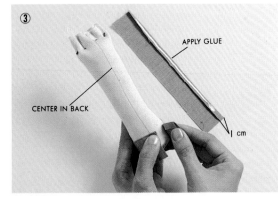

③ Turn 1 cm edge of oblong piece to wrong side, apply glue on it. Wrap the piece round the foot, turn the end at back to wrong side, pin to steady. Finish in fine slip-stitches with fabric color thread.

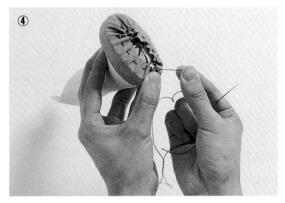

④ Hand-stitch along the edge with No. 8 machine thread doubled, overcasting crosswise, secue the end.

⑤ Pin felt sole to the base and sew on, working with fine slip-stitches.

⑥ Finished foot.

⑦ Put the finished legs together, join at the top taking a stitch to make their length the same.

10 TO SEW EACH SECTION ON THE BODY:

Check each section to see if the work is correctly done, then sew on to the body.

① Sew legs firmly on body front with 2 strands of No. 8 machine thread.

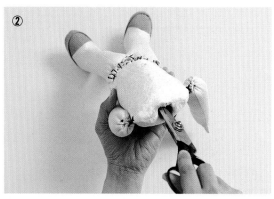

② Sew arms on body with a shank as button-sewing. Make a hole at the top of the body at right angles to the seam line; put scissors in and turn to enlarge to neck size.

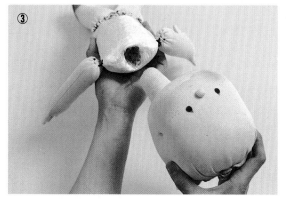

③ Insert the neck.

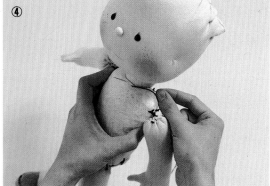

④ Stitch firmly (so the head doesn't totter) to the body, bringing the needle through the middle of the neck to the front with 2 strands of No. 8 machine thread.

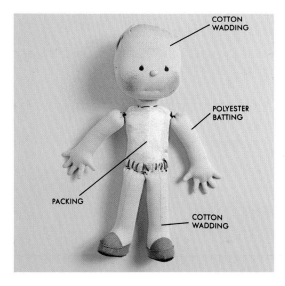

COTTON WADDING

POLYESTER BATTING

PACKING

COTTON WADDING

STUFFING MATERIALS:

Use three types of stuffing materials, packing, cotton wadding, and polyester batting to make the different part of the doll.

- Packing is strips of wooden shavings mainly used to form a head-foundation and body which finish has to be firm and solid.
- Cotton wadding is mainly used for the face, fingers, and legs which have to be finished softly and yet firmly. To get the sizes needed, tear off pieces roughly with hand instead of using scissors.
- Polyester batting is a convenient material, for it is springy without becoming bulky. Mainly used for the parts of amrs and legs where wanted to be formed softly.

11 TO SEW CLOTHES:

Doll's clothes are partly sewn beforehand, then each garment completed by sewing it to the body.

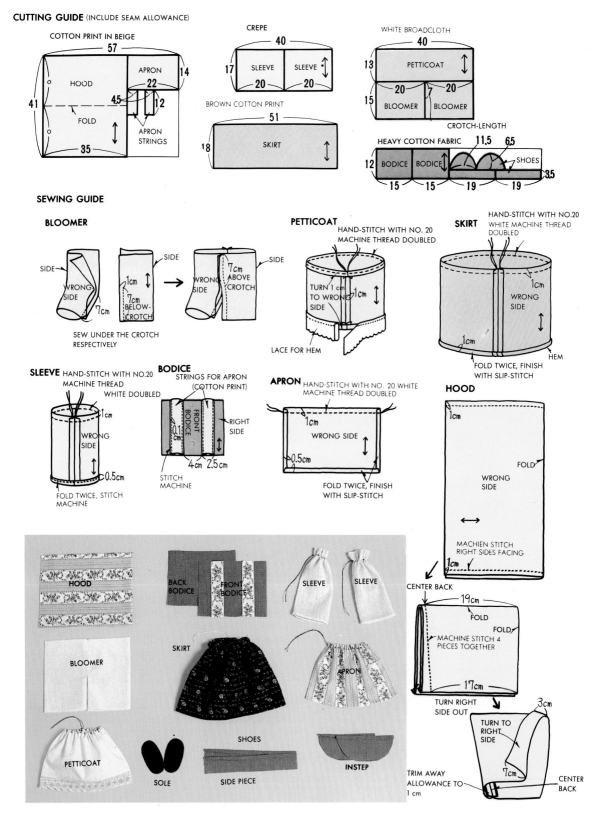

CUTTING GUIDE (INCLUDE SEAM ALLOWANCE)

COTTON PRINT IN BEIGE
57
HOOD
APRON 22 14
41 45 12
FOLD
35 APRON STRINGS

CREPE
40
17 SLEEVE SLEEVE
20 20

BROWN COTTON PRINT
51
18 SKIRT

WHITE BROADCLOTH
40
13 PETTICOAT
15 20 20
BLOOMER BLOOMER
CROTCH-LENGTH

HEAVY COTTON FABRIC 11.5 6.5
12 BODICE BODICE SHOES 3.5
15 15 19 19

SEWING GUIDE

BLOOMER
SIDE
SIDE
WRONG SIDE
7cm
SIDE
1cm
7cm BELOW CROTCH
WRONG SIDE
7cm ABOVE CROTCH
SIDE
SIDE
SEW UNDER THE CROTCH RESPECTIVELY

PETTICOAT
HAND-STITCH WITH NO. 20 MACHINE THREAD DOUBLED
TURN 1 cm TO WRONG SIDE
1cm
LACE FOR HEM

SKIRT
HAND-STITCH WITH NO.20 WHITE MACHINE THREAD DOUBLED
1cm
WRONG SIDE
1cm
HEM
FOLD TWICE, FINISH WITH SLIP-STITCH

SLEEVE
HAND-STITCH WITH NO.20 MACHINE THREAD WHITE DOUBLED
1cm
WRONG SIDE
0.5cm
FOLD TWICE, STITCH MACHINE

BODICE
STRINGS FOR APRON (COTTON PRINT)
FRONT BODICE
0.1cm
RIGHT SIDE
4cm 2.5cm
STITCH MACHINE

APRON
HAND-STITCH WITH NO. 20 WHITE MACHINE THREAD DOUBLED
1cm
WRONG SIDE
0.5cm
FOLD TWICE, FINISH WITH SLIP-STITCH

HOOD
1cm
WRONG SIDE
FOLD
1cm
MACHIEN STITCH RIGHT SIDES FACING
CENTER BACK
19cm
FOLD
FOLD
MACHINE STITCH 4 PIECES TOGETHER
17cm
TURN RIGHT SIDE OUT
3cm
TURN TO RIGHT SIDE
7cm
TRIM AWAY ALLOWANCE TO 1 cm
CENTER BACK

HOOD

BACK BODICE FRONT BODICE

SLEEVE SLEEVE

BLOOMER

SKIRT

APRON

PETTICOAT

SOLE

SIDE PIECE

SHOES

INSTEP

12 TO SEW ON CLOTHES:

Sew on underwear first. Conceal cut ends or seam allowances with overlapped piece. Work fine stitches neatly where seen from outside.

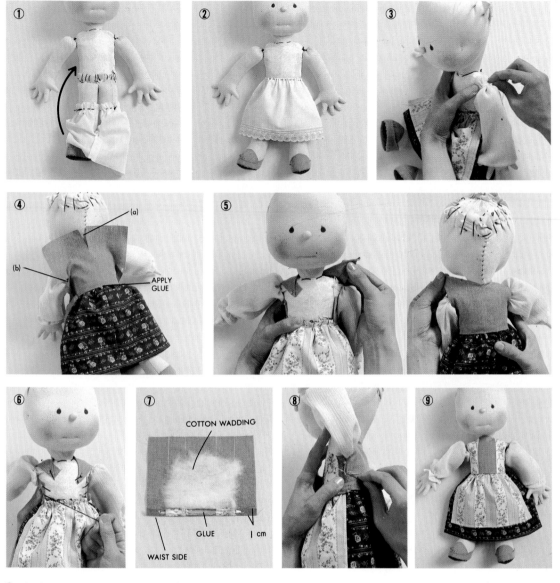

① Having drawn up lower ends of the bloomers, turn up waist section. Tuck at four places and secure. Put on petticoat, draw gather, and sew on body.

② Put skirt over petticoat, draw gather slightly above waist of petticoat, overlay apron and secure to the body.

③ Put sleeves on arms, stitch and gather at top, secure to shoulders. Gather sleeve-ends, stitching 1 cm from edge.

④ Turn lower edge of bodice back 1 cm to wrong side, apply glue. Put it over the allowance of the skirt, pin sides firmly. Clip at (a) & (b).

⑤ Turn the allowance at neck and arms to wrong side, pin the pieces from shoulders and sides to body front.

⑥ Stitch to the body with 2 strands of No. 8 machine thread.

⑦ Lay thin wadding piece on the wrong side of front bodice.

⑧ Put the piece on the body front turning allowances to wrong side, secure sides and shoulders working in fine slip-stitches with sewing thread.

⑨ Clothed doll.

13 TO SEW ON HAIR AND CAP:

Make a bundle of yarn 160 cm long (the same length as the skein of yarn clipped at the center). Put it on the head, smoothing with a coarse tooth comb.
Secure yarns following the arrows on the chart.

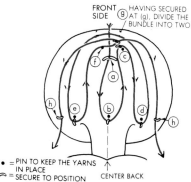

FRONT SIDE
(g) HAVING SECURED AT (g), DIVIDE THE BUNDLE INTO TWO

● = PIN TO KEEP THE YARNS IN PLACE
⌒ = SECURE TO POSITION
CENTER BACK

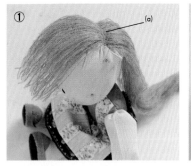

① Put front hair down on forehead, adjusting to the width of face. Steady with yarn carried across top (a) and slightly backward.

② Pin at the center back (b), bring yarn up to (c).

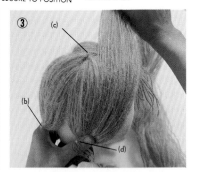

③ Pin at (c) & (d), place yarn as in (2). Pass the yarn to (e), putting widely along the outline of the face.

④ Having carried yarn across to point (g), secure at each point after (g) is secured to head.

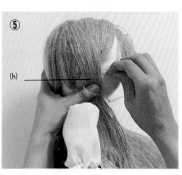

⑤ Divide the remaining yarn in two, and bring down on both sides, secure at (h).

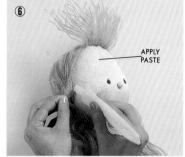

APPLY PASTE

⑥ Apply paste on forehead and at position of ears, attach yarn to the skin-fabric.

RIBBON

⑦ Trim front hair evenly. Braid yarn on both sides, secure ends with ribbon.

⑧ Place cap on head, secure above the front hair and at neck back with glue.

Completed Hiji.

CLARA

Shown on front cover.

A scalloped lace used for her dress, but you may use a fabric trimmed with lace instead.

YOU'LL NEED:

Head-Foundation, Body, Arms, Legs—90 cm by 21 cm white rayon. Face, Nose, Arms—45 cm by 25 cm beige cotton jersey. Legs—36 cm by 21 cm white jersey. Eyes—dacron georgette. Mouth—strands of embroidery thread. Hair—bouclé. Bloomer, Petticoat—80 cm by 18 cm white broadcloth, 40 cm of 3.5 cm lace, 50 cm of 3 cm lace. Dress, Cap—15 cm by 310 cm cotton lace fabric, 50 cm of 0.6 cm ribbon. Shoes—36 cm of 1.5 cm lace, 11 cm by 5 cm felt. Also—packing, cotton wadding, polyester batting.

FINISHED SIZE; Refer to diagram.
INSTRUCTIONS:

The basic method is the same as for Hiji, so refer to pages 50-64.

Make legs up to knee as for Hiji.

Make dress and cap with length of scalloped lace fabric.

Make hair by winding ringlets of yarn round a finger, secure each to head with machine thread, leaving proper space between. Secure to head all over without clipping the yarn following.

① PATTERNS (ACTUAL SIZE):

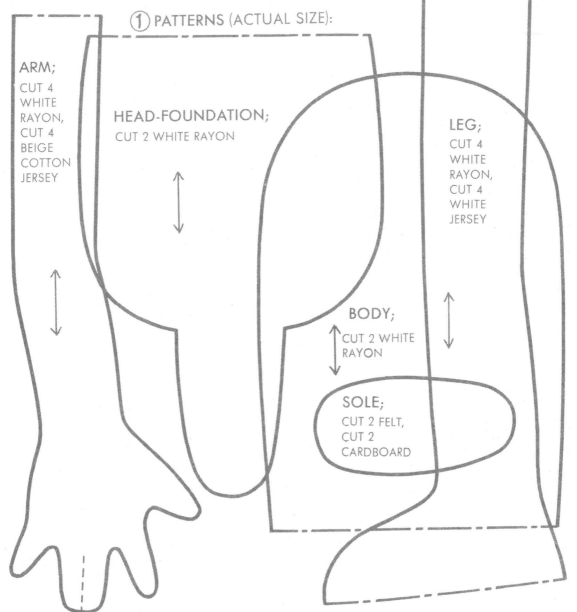

ARM;
CUT 4 WHITE RAYON,
CUT 4 BEIGE COTTON JERSEY

HEAD-FOUNDATION;
CUT 2 WHITE RAYON

LEG;
CUT 4 WHITE RAYON,
CUT 4 WHITE JERSEY

BODY;
CUT 2 WHITE RAYON

SOLE;
CUT 2 FELT,
CUT 2 CARDBOARD

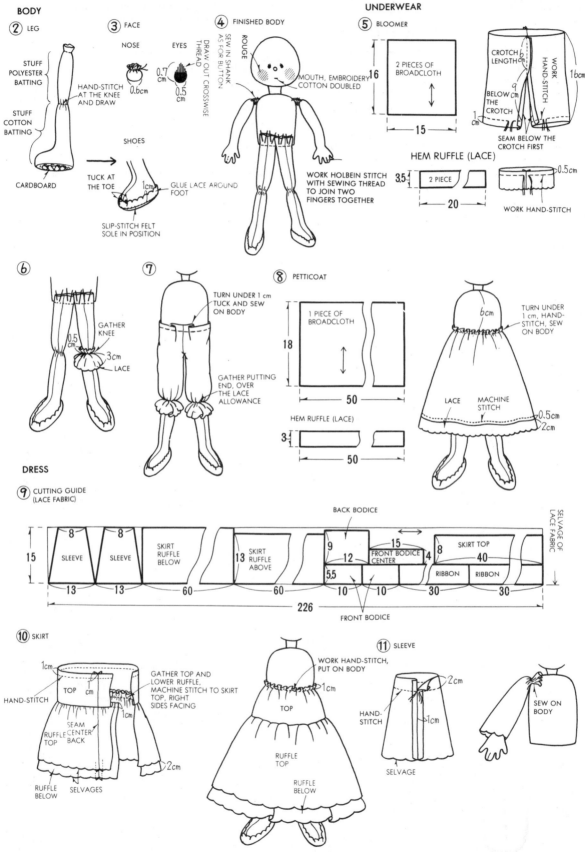

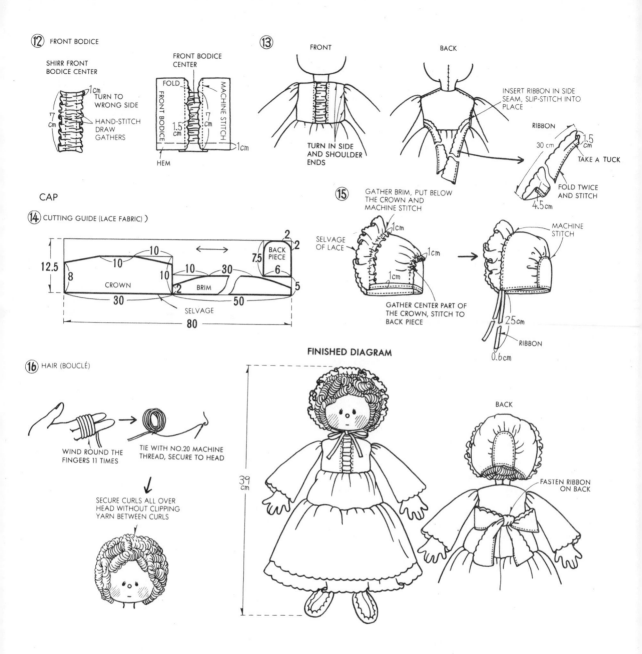

⑫ FRONT BODICE

SHIRR FRONT
BODICE CENTER

1cm
TURN TO
WRONG SIDE

7
cm

HAND-STITCH
DRAW
GATHERS

FRONT BODICE
CENTER

FOLD
FRONT BODICE

MACHINE STITCH

1.5
cm

7
cm

HEM

1cm

⑬ FRONT   BACK

TURN IN SIDE
AND SHOULDER
ENDS

INSERT RIBBON IN SIDE
SEAM, SLIP-STITCH INTO
PLACE

RIBBON

30 cm

1.5
cm

TAKE A TUCK

FOLD TWICE
AND STITCH

4.5cm

CAP

⑭ CUTTING GUIDE (LACE FABRIC))

12.5

8

CROWN

10

10

10

30

10

10

2

BRIM

30

50

SELVAGE

80

2
2

BACK
PIECE

7.5

6

5

⑮ GATHER BRIM, PUT BELOW
THE CROWN AND
MACHINE STITCH

SELVAGE
OF LACE

1cm

1cm

1cm

GATHER CENTER PART OF
THE CROWN, STITCH TO
BACK PIECE

MACHINE
STITCH

25cm

RIBBON

0.6cm

⑯ HAIR (BOUCLÉ)

WIND ROUND THE
FINGERS 11 TIMES

TIE WITH NO.20 MACHINE
THREAD, SECURE TO HEAD

SECURE CURLS ALL OVER
HEAD WITHOUT CLIPPING
YARN BETWEEN CURLS

FINISHED DIAGRAM

39
cm

BACK

FASTEN RIBBON
ON BACK

YOU'LL NEED:
YOU'LL NEED:
Head-Foundation, Body, Arms, Legs—70 cm by 35 cm
white rayon. Face, Nose, Arms, Legs—50 cm by 40 cm
cotton jersey. Eyes—dacron georgette. Mouth—strands of
embroidery thread. Hair—bouclé, 75 cm of 7 cm lace
ribbon. Bloomer, Dress—90 cm by 40 cm cotton print, 56
cm of 3 cm lace, 270 cm of 2.5 cm lace. Also—packing,
cotton wadding, polyester batting.
FINISHED SIZE; Refer to diagram.

INSTRUCTIONS:
The basic method is the same as for Hiji, so refer to pages
50-64.
Make legs stuffing polyester batting in same manner as for
hands and finish openings the same way.
Having stitched decorative piece of front bodice and lace
together, sew on body. Hand-stitch along the neck, gather
and secure at back.
Sew on hair as for Red-Riding Hood on page 72, trim the
ends evenly.

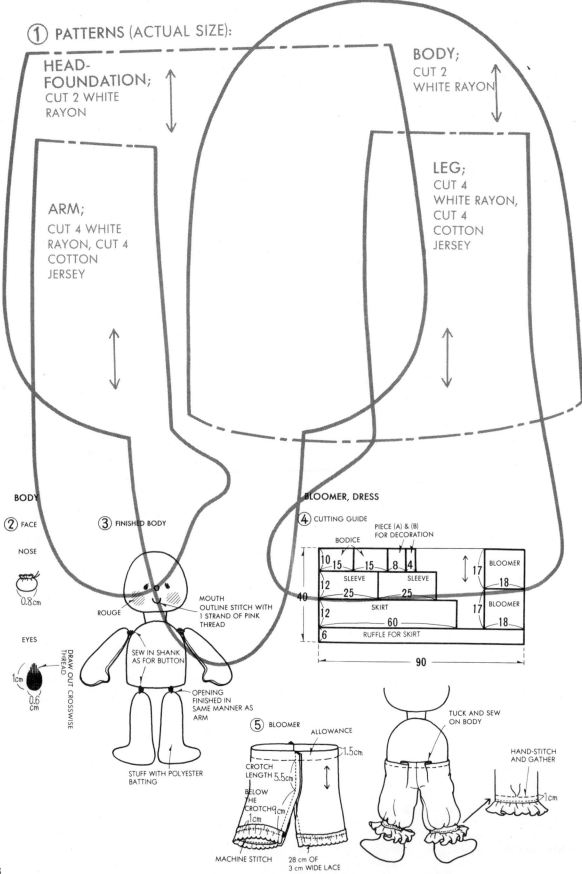

① PATTERNS (ACTUAL SIZE):

HEAD-FOUNDATION;
CUT 2 WHITE RAYON

BODY;
CUT 2 WHITE RAYON

ARM;
CUT 4 WHITE RAYON, CUT 4 COTTON JERSEY

LEG;
CUT 4 WHITE RAYON, CUT 4 COTTON JERSEY

BODY

② FACE

NOSE

0.8cm

ROUGE

MOUTH
OUTLINE STITCH WITH 1 STRAND OF PINK THREAD

EYES

DRAW OUT CROSSWISE THREAD

1cm

0.6cm

③ FINISHED BODY

SEW IN SHANK AS FOR BUTTON

OPENING FINISHED IN SAME MANNER AS ARM

STUFF WITH POLYESTER BATTING

BLOOMER, DRESS

④ CUTTING GUIDE

PIECE (A) & (B) FOR DECORATION

BODICE

| 10 | 15 | | 15 | | 8 | 4 | | | 17 | BLOOMER |

SLEEVE   SLEEVE

12   25   25   18

40

SKIRT   17   BLOOMER

12   60   18

6   RUFFLE FOR SKIRT

90

⑤ BLOOMER

ALLOWANCE

1.5cm

CROTCH LENGTH 5.5cm

BELOW THE CROTCH 1cm

1cm

MACHINE STITCH

28 cm OF 3 cm WIDE LACE

TUCK AND SEW ON BODY

HAND-STITCH AND GATHER

1cm

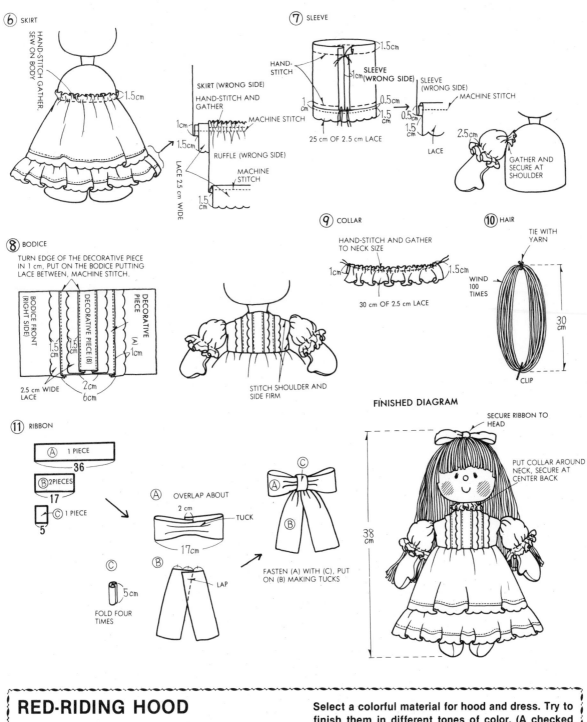

⑥ SKIRT

HAND-STITCH GATHER,
SEW ON BODY

1.5cm

SKIRT (WRONG SIDE)

HAND-STITCH AND
GATHER

1cm

1.5cm

MACHINE STITCH

RUFFLE (WRONG SIDE)

MACHINE
STITCH

LACE 2.5 cm WIDE

1.5cm

LACE 2.5 cm WIDE

⑦ SLEEVE

1.5cm

HAND-STITCH

1cm

SLEEVE (WRONG SIDE)

0.5cm

1.5cm

25 cm OF 2.5 cm LACE

SLEEVE (WRONG SIDE)

MACHINE STITCH

0.5cm

1.5cm

LACE

2.5cm

GATHER AND
SECURE AT
SHOULDER

⑧ BODICE

TURN EDGE OF THE DECORATIVE PIECE
IN 1 cm, PUT ON THE BODICE PUTTING
LACE BETWEEN, MACHINE STITCH.

BODICE FRONT (RIGHT SIDE)

DECORATIVE PIECE (B)

DECORATIVE PIECE (A)

1.5cm   1.5cm   1cm

2cm

6cm

2.5 cm WIDE LACE

STITCH SHOULDER AND
SIDE FIRM

⑨ COLLAR

HAND-STITCH AND GATHER
TO NECK SIZE

1cm

1.5cm

30 cm OF 2.5 cm LACE

⑩ HAIR

TIE WITH YARN

WIND 100 TIMES

30 cm

CLIP

⑪ RIBBON

Ⓐ 1 PIECE
36

Ⓑ 2 PIECES
17

Ⓒ 1 PIECE
5

OVERLAP ABOUT
2 cm

TUCK

17cm

Ⓒ
5cm

FOLD FOUR TIMES

Ⓑ

LAP

FASTEN (A) WITH (C), PUT
ON (B) MAKING TUCKS

Ⓒ
Ⓐ
Ⓑ

FINISHED DIAGRAM

SECURE RIBBON TO HEAD

PUT COLLAR AROUND
NECK, SECURE AT
CENTER BACK

38 cm

RED-RIDING HOOD

Shown on page 3.

Select a colorful material for hood and dress. Try to finish them in different tones of color. (A checked fabric hood and apron might also be pretty.)

YOU'LL NEED:
Head-Foundation, Body, Arms, Legs—55 cm by 52cm white rayon. Face, Nose, Arms, Legs—65 cm by 52 cm cotton jersey. Eyes—dacron georgette. Mouth—strands of embroidery thread. Hair—sport-weight yarn, 40 cm of 0.3 cm ribbon. Bloomer, Petticoat—90 cm by 20 cm white broadcloth, 50 cm of 2 cm lace. Dress—82 cm by 37 cm seersucker. Vest—19 cm by 13 cm orange felt, ogrnge strands of embroidery thread. Apron—41 cm by 100 cm seersucker. Hood—22 cm by 45 cm red felt. Shoes—20 cm by 17 cm gray felt, Gray embroidery thread. Also—packing, cotton wadding, polyester batting.
FINISHED SIZE: Refer to diagram.

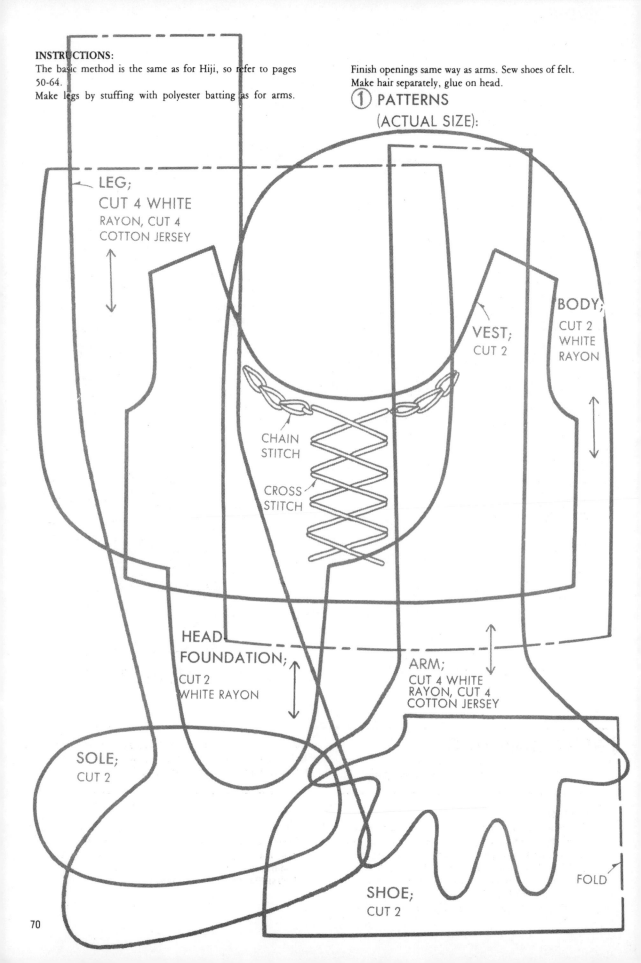

INSTRUCTIONS:
The basic method is the same as for Hiji, so refer to pages 50-64.
Make legs by stuffing with polyester batting as for arms.

Finish openings same way as arms. Sew shoes of felt.
Make hair separately, glue on head.

① PATTERNS
(ACTUAL SIZE):

LEG;
CUT 4 WHITE
RAYON, CUT 4
COTTON JERSEY

BODY;
CUT 2
WHITE
RAYON

VEST;
CUT 2

CHAIN
STITCH

CROSS
STITCH

HEAD
FOUNDATION;
CUT 2
WHITE RAYON

ARM;
CUT 4 WHITE
RAYON, CUT 4
COTTON JERSEY

SOLE;
CUT 2

SHOE;
CUT 2

FOLD

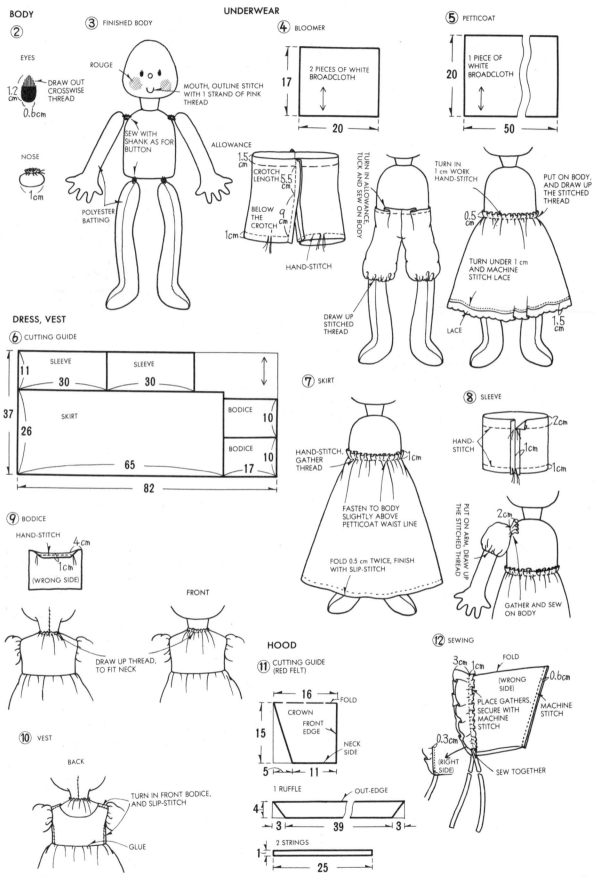

BODY

②

EYES

1.2 cm
0.6cm

DRAW OUT CROSSWISE THREAD

NOSE

1cm

③ FINISHED BODY

ROUGE

MOUTH, OUTLINE STITCH WITH 1 STRAND OF PINK THREAD

SEW WITH SHANK AS FOR BUTTON

ALLOWANCE

POLYESTER BATTING

UNDERWEAR

④ BLOOMER

2 PIECES OF WHITE BROADCLOTH

17
20

⑤ PETTICOAT

1 PIECE OF WHITE BROADCLOTH

20
50

1.5 cm
CROTCH LENGTH 5.5 cm
BELOW THE CROTCH
9 cm
1cm

HAND-STITCH

TURN IN ALLOWANCE, TUCK AND SEW ON BODY

TURN IN 1 cm WORK HAND-STITCH

DRAW UP STITCHED THREAD

PUT ON BODY, AND DRAW UP THE STITCHED THREAD

0.5 cm

TURN UNDER 1 cm AND MACHINE STITCH LACE

LACE

1.5 cm

DRESS, VEST

⑥ CUTTING GUIDE

11
SLEEVE 30
SLEEVE 30
37
26
SKIRT
BODICE 10
BODICE 10
65
17
82

⑦ SKIRT

HAND-STITCH, GATHER THREAD

1cm

FASTEN TO BODY SLIGHTLY ABOVE PETTICOAT WAIST LINE

FOLD 0.5 cm TWICE, FINISH WITH SLIP-STITCH

⑧ SLEEVE

2cm
HAND-STITCH
1cm
1cm

PUT ON ARM, DRAW UP THE STITCHED THREAD

2cm

GATHER AND SEW ON BODY

⑨ BODICE

HAND-STITCH
4 cm
1cm
(WRONG SIDE)

FRONT

DRAW UP THREAD, TO FIT NECK

⑩ VEST

BACK

TURN IN FRONT BODICE, AND SLIP-STITCH

GLUE

HOOD

⑪ CUTTING GUIDE (RED FELT)

16
FOLD
CROWN
FRONT EDGE
15
NECK SIDE
5
11

1 RUFFLE
OUT-EDGE
4
3
39
3

2 STRINGS
1
25

⑫ SEWING

3cm 1cm
FOLD
(WRONG SIDE)
0.6cm
PLACE GATHERS, SECURE WITH MACHINE STITCH
MACHINE STITCH
0.3cm
(RIGHT SIDE)
SEW TOGETHER

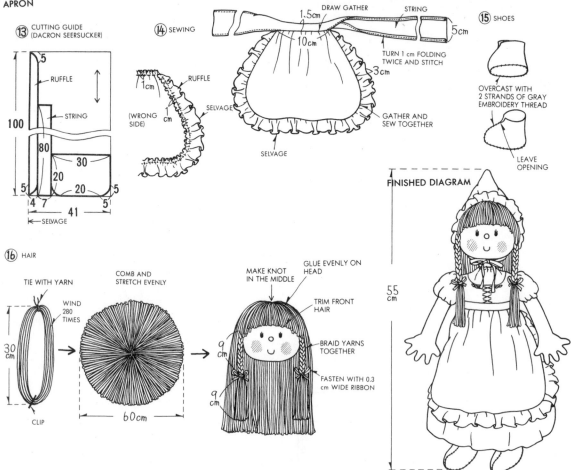

APRON

⑬ CUTTING GUIDE (DACRON SEERSUCKER)

RUFFLE
STRING
100
80
30
20
20
5 — 4 7 — 41 — 5
SELVAGE

⑭ SEWING

1cm
(WRONG SIDE)
RUFFLE
cm
SELVAGE
SELVAGE

DRAW GATHER STRING
1.5cm
10cm
5cm
TURN 1 CM FOLDING TWICE AND STITCH
3cm
GATHER AND SEW TOGETHER

⑮ SHOES

OVERCAST WITH 2 STRANDS OF GRAY EMBROIDERY THREAD
LEAVE OPENING

FINISHED DIAGRAM

55 cm

⑯ HAIR

TIE WITH YARN
WIND 280 TIMES
30 cm
CLIP

COMB AND STRETCH EVENLY
60cm

MAKE KNOT IN THE MIDDLE
GLUE EVENLY ON HEAD
TRIM FRONT HAIR
BRAID YARNS TOGETHER
FASTEN WITH 0.3 cm WIDE RIBBON
9 cm
9 cm

KAREN

Shown on page 2.

The hat on her head is ready-made. You may crochet one of raffia, adjusting it to her head shape (refer to page 156). Felt way also be used for shoes.

YOU'LL NEED:
Head-Foundation, Body, Arms, Legs—90 cm by 60 cm white rayon. Face, Nose, Arms, Chest—65 cm by 30 cm cotton jersey. Legs—22 cm by 37 cm bleached cotton. Eyes—dacron georgette. Mouth—strands of embroidery thread. Hair-mohair yarn. Bloomer, Petticoat—80 cm by 51 cm white dacron georgette, 145 cm of 5.5 cm lace. Dress—90 cm by 240 cm nylon lace, 24 cm by 21 cm bleached cotton, 100 cm of 0.7 cm satin ribbon. Shoes—21 cm by 10 cm red suede. Also—packing, cotton wadding, polyester batting, hat.

FINISHED SIZE: Refer to diagram.
INSTRUCTIONS:
The basic method is the same as for Hiji, so refer to pages 50-64.
Finish the openings of legs as for arms. Put bodice on the body, laying bleached cotton underneath. Sew on sleeves and skirt with the fabric folded in half.
Put on skirt with seam lines on center back, sides in front.
Attach hair as shown above, trimming front hair evenly.

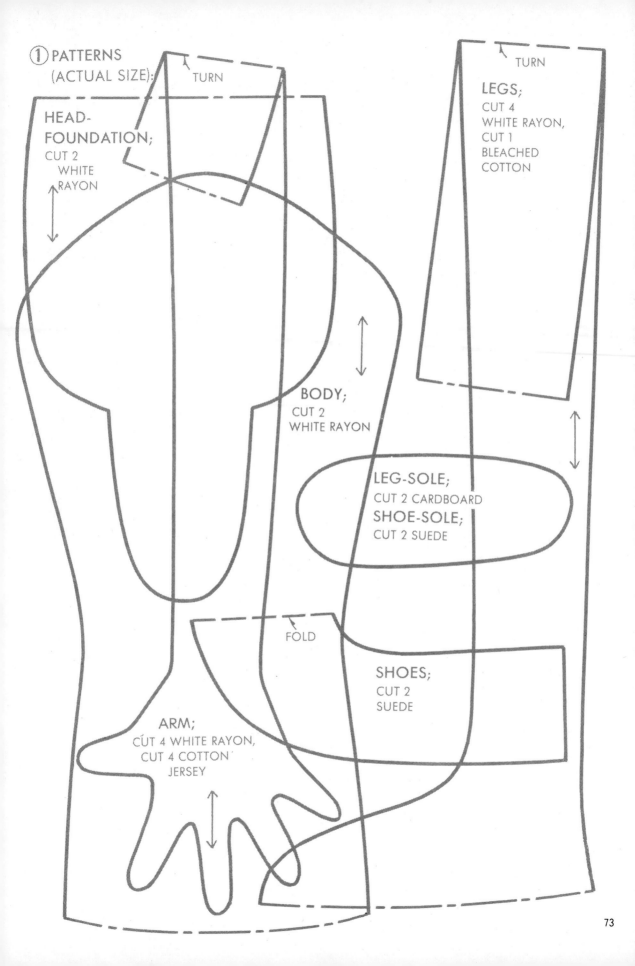

① PATTERNS
(ACTUAL SIZE):

TURN

HEAD-
FOUNDATION;
CUT 2
    WHITE
    RAYON

TURN

LEGS;
CUT 4
WHITE RAYON,
CUT 1
BLEACHED
COTTON

BODY;
CUT 2
WHITE RAYON

LEG-SOLE;
CUT 2 CARDBOARD
SHOE-SOLE;
CUT 2 SUEDE

FOLD

SHOES;
CUT 2
SUEDE

ARM;
CUT 4 WHITE RAYON,
CUT 4 COTTON
JERSEY

73

BODY

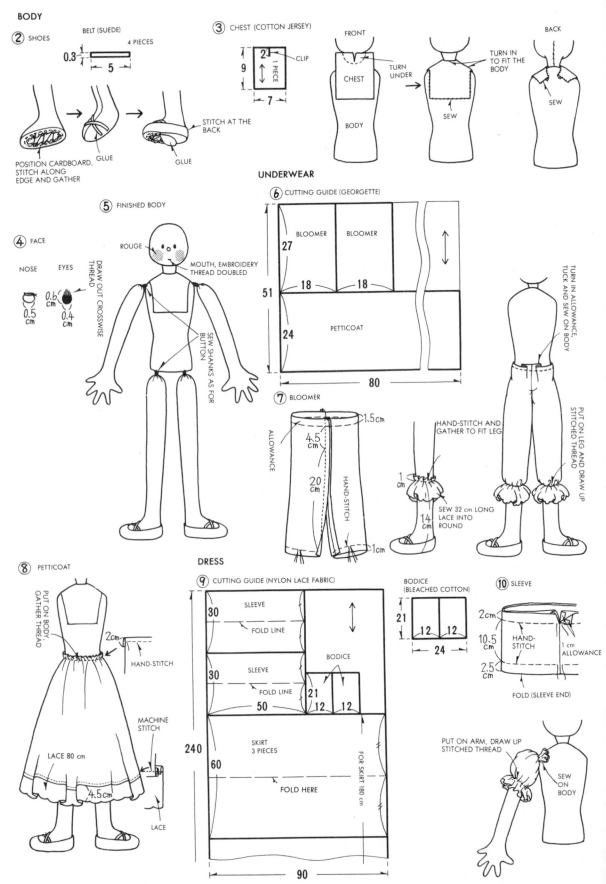

BODY

② SHOES

BELT (SUEDE)

4 PIECES

0.3

5

POSITION CARDBOARD, STITCH ALONG EDGE AND GATHER

GLUE

GLUE

STITCH AT THE BACK

③ CHEST (COTTON JERSEY)

2

9

7

1 PIECE

CLIP

FRONT

CHEST

BODY

TURN UNDER

TURN IN TO FIT THE BODY

SEW

BACK

SEW

⑤ FINISHED BODY

④ FACE

ROUGE

MOUTH, EMBROIDERY THREAD DOUBLED

NOSE

0.5 cm

EYES

0.6 cm

0.4 cm

DRAW OUT CROSSWISE THREAD

SEW SHANKS AS FOR BUTTON

UNDERWEAR

⑥ CUTTING GUIDE (GEORGETTE)

27

51

24

BLOOMER

BLOOMER

18

18

PETTICOAT

80

TURN IN ALLOWANCE, TUCK AND SEW ON BODY

⑦ BLOOMER

ALLOWANCE

1.5 cm

4.5 cm

20 cm

HAND-STITCH

HAND-STITCH AND GATHER TO FIT LEG

1 cm

14 cm

SEW 32 cm LONG LACE INTO ROUND

1 cm

PUT ON LEG AND DRAW UP STITCHED THREAD

DRESS

⑧ PETTICOAT

PUT ON BODY, GATHER THREAD

2 cm

HAND-STITCH

MACHINE STITCH

LACE 80 cm

4.5 cm

LACE

⑨ CUTTING GUIDE (NYLON LACE FABRIC)

30

SLEEVE

FOLD LINE

30

SLEEVE

FOLD LINE

50

BODICE

21

12

12

SKIRT 3 PIECES

240

60

FOLD HERE

FOR SKIRT 180 cm

90

BODICE (BLEACHED COTTON)

21

12

12

24

⑩ SLEEVE

2 cm

10.5 cm

HAND-STITCH

1 cm ALLOWANCE

2.5 cm

FOLD (SLEEVE END)

PUT ON ARM, DRAW UP STITCHED THREAD

SEW ON BODY

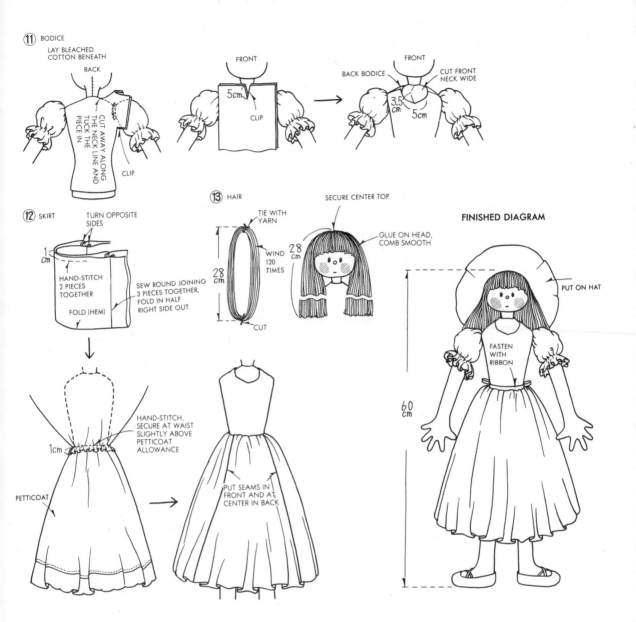

(11) BODICE

LAY BLEACHED COTTON BENEATH

BACK

CUT AWAY ALONG THE NECK LINE AND TUCK THE PIECE IN

CLIP

FRONT

5cm

CLIP

FRONT

BACK BODICE

CUT FRONT NECK WIDE

3.5 cm

5cm

(12) SKIRT

TURN OPPOSITE SIDES

1 cm

HAND-STITCH 2 PIECES TOGETHER

SEW ROUND JOINING 3 PIECES TOGETHER, FOLD IN HALF RIGHT SIDE OUT

FOLD (HEM)

(13) HAIR

TIE WITH YARN

SECURE CENTER TOP

GLUE ON HEAD, COMB SMOOTH

WIND 120 TIMES

28 cm

28 cm

CUT

FINISHED DIAGRAM

PUT ON HAT

FASTEN WITH RIBBON

60 cm

HAND-STITCH, SECURE AT WAIST SLIGHTLY ABOVE PETTICOAT ALLOWANCE

1cm

PETTICOAT

PUT SEAMS IN FRONT AND AT CENTER IN BACK

LITTLE HOUSE IN THE BIG WOODS

Shown on pages 4—5.

Use denim, calico, and homespun for an old-fashioned look for this pioneer family.

(MARY)

YOU'LL NEED:
Head-Foundation, Body, Arms, Legs—90 cm by 18 cm white rayon. Face, Nose, Arms—32 cm by 17 cm beige cotton jersey. Legs—28 cm black cotton jersey. Eyes—dacron georgette. Mouth—strands of embroidery thread. Hair—mohair yarn. Bloomer, Petticoat—60 cm by 17 cm white rayon. Skirt, Sleeves, Bonnet—63 cm by 30 cm denim. Apron-Dress—43 cm by 23 cm cotton print. Shoes—12 cm by 6 cm felt. Also—packing, cotton wadding, polyester batting.

FINISHED SIZE: Refer to diagram.
INSTRUCTIONS:
The basic method is the same as for Hiji, so refer to pages 50-64.
Make legs in same manner as for arms.
Seam sides of apron-dress, press seams open, finish the hem.
Secure hair at center of head, glue and comb smooth.
Make shoes to fit size of foot.

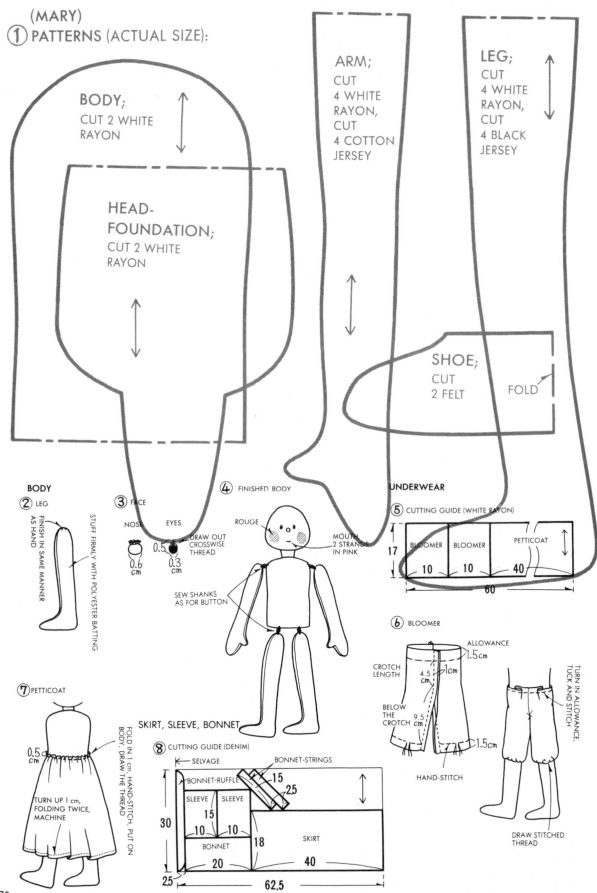

(MARY)
① PATTERNS (ACTUAL SIZE):

BODY;
CUT 2 WHITE
RAYON

HEAD-
FOUNDATION;
CUT 2 WHITE
RAYON

ARM;
CUT
4 WHITE
RAYON,
CUT
4 COTTON
JERSEY

LEG;
CUT
4 WHITE
RAYON,
CUT
4 BLACK
JERSEY

SHOE;
CUT
2 FELT
FOLD

BODY

② LEG
STUFF FIRMLY WITH POLYESTER BATTING
FINISH IN SAME MANNER AS HAND

③ FACE
NOSE   EYES
0.6 cm   0.5   0.3 cm
DRAW OUT CROSSWISE THREAD

④ FINISHED BODY
ROUGE
MOUTH
2 STRANDS
IN PINK
SEW SHANKS
AS FOR BUTTON

UNDERWEAR

⑤ CUTTING GUIDE (WHITE RAYON)
17
BLOOMER BLOOMER PETTICOAT
10   10   40
60

⑥ BLOOMER
CROTCH
LENGTH
4.5 cm   1cm
BELOW
THE
CROTCH   9.5 cm
ALLOWANCE
1.5cm
TURN IN ALLOWANCE,
TUCK AND STITCH
1.5cm
HAND-STITCH
DRAW STITCHED
THREAD

⑦ PETTICOAT
0.5 cm
TURN UP 1 cm,
FOLDING TWICE,
MACHINE
FOLD IN 1 cm, HAND-STITCH, PUT ON
BODY, DRAW THE THREAD

SKIRT, SLEEVE, BONNET
⑧ CUTTING GUIDE (DENIM)
SELVAGE
BONNET-STRINGS
BONNET-RUFFLE   15
2.5
SLEEVE SLEEVE
15
10   10
30
BONNET
18
20
25
62.5
SKIRT
40

(9) SKIRT

HAND-STITCH

HAND-STITCH, PETTICOAT AND GATHER

TURN UP 1.5 cm, FOLDING TWICE, SLIP-STITCH

(10) SLEEVE

1cm
1.5cm

HAND-STITCH

TURN 1.5 cm FOLDING TWICE, SLIP-STITCH

GATHER AND SEW ON BODY

(11) BONNET

2cm

GATHER RUFFLE, MACHINE STITCH

1.5cm

TURN THE EDGE, HAND-STITCH AND GATHER

SWE STRING HERE

TURN 1 cm FOLDING TWICE, SLIP-STITCH

STRING

0.6cm

STITCH THEN TURN INSIDEN OUT

(12) APRON-DRESS

BODICE FRONT AND BACK (CUT 2 COTTON PRINT)

23

21.5

2.5cm
4cm
1.5cm
1cm
3.5cm

STITCH-END

FINE HAND-STITCHES

0.5 cm

BODICE FRONT (WRONG SIDE)

STITCH, PRESS OPEN

TURN 1.5 cm FOLDING TWICE, SLIP-STITCH

(13) HAIR

TIE LOOSELY

WIND 120 TIMES

25 cm

CUT

4.5cm

STEADY WITH 1 STRAND OF MOHAIR YARN

APPLY GLUE ON HEAD, POSITION YARN

25cm

DRAW THREAD UP TO FIT THE NECK

JOIN AT SHOULDER

DRAW FITTING TO THE BODY

(14) SHOES

FOLD

FINE SLIP-STITCH ALONG EDGE

FINISHED DIAGRAM

35 cm

(LAURA)

YOU'LL NEED:

Head-Foundation, Body, Arms, Legs—84 cm by 17 cm white rayon. Face, Nose, Arms—32 cm by 15 cm beige cotton jersey. Legs—26 cm by 17 cm black cotton jersey. Eyes—dacron georgette. Mouth—strands of embroidery thread. Hair-mohair yarn. Bloomer, Petticoat—60 cm by 15 cm white rayon. Skirt—45 cm by 16 cm lightweight cotton fabric. Dress, Bonnet—67 cm by 30 cm cotton print.

Shoes—11 cm by 5.5 cm felt. Also—packing, cotton wadding, polyester batting.

FINISHED SIZE: Refer to diagram.

INSTRUCTIONS:

The basic method is the same as for Hiji, so refer to pages 50-60, and made in same manner as Mary.

Secure hair on top left side, cut the ends evenly.

(LAURA)
① PATTERNS (ACTUAL SIZE):

BODY;
CUT 2 WHITE RAYON

HEAD-FOUNDATION;
CUT 2 WHITE RAYON

ARM;
CUT
4 WHITE
RAYON,
CUT
4 BEIGE
COTTON
JERSEY

LEG;
CUT 4
WHITE
RAYON,
CUT 4
BEIGE
COTTON
JERSEY

SHOE;
CUT
2 FELT

FOLD

BODY

② FACE

NOSE

0.5cm

EYES

0.5 cm 0.3 cm

ROUGE

DRAW OUT CROSSWISE THREAD

FRECKLES

MOUTH, OUTLINE STITCH 1 STRAND PINK

UNDERWEAR

③ CUTTING GUIDE (WHITE RAYON)

BLOOMER	BLOOMER	PETTICOAT
10	10	40

15

60

④ BLOOMER

ALLOWANCE 1.5cm

3.5 cm 10m

CROTCH LENGTH

BELOW THE CROTCH 8.5 cm

1.5 cm

HAND-STITCH

DRESS, BONNET

⑤ CUTTING GUIDE

SKIRT (LIGHTWEIGHT COTTON)

SKIRT	
40	25

16

45

DRESS, BONNET (COTTON PRINT)

BONNET RUFFLE

BONNET-STRINGS

SELVAGE

SLEEVE 13
SLEEVE
10 10 21

BONNET 10

20

BODICE

BODICE

30

2.5

22 22

66.5

⑥ DRESS

SLEEVE

ALLOWANCE 1.5cm

HAND-STITCH

0.5 cm

TURN 1 cm FOLDING TWICE, SLIP-STITCH

BODICE

2.5cm 1cm

4cm

3.5cm

1.5 cm

FINE HAND-STITCHES

(WRONG SIDE)

0.5cm

STITCH, PRESS SEAM OPEN

TURN 1 cm FOLDING TWICE, SLIP-STITCH

⑦ HAIR

WORK AS FOR MARY

4cm

SECURE AT LEFT TOP WITH 1 STRAND OF MOHAIR YARN

FINISHED DIAGRAM

32 cm

TRIM EVENLY

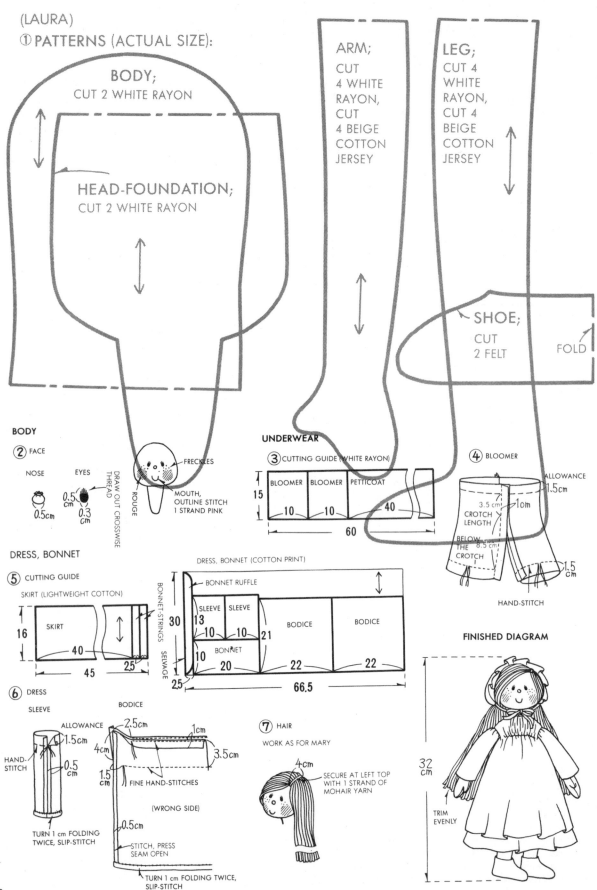

(CARRIE)

YOU'LL NEED:

Head-Foundation, Body, Arms, Legs—60 cm by 12 cm white rayon. Face, Nose Arms, Legs—30 cm by 20 cm cotton jersey. Eyes—dacron georgette. Mouth—strands of embroidery thread. Hair—mohair yarn. Shoes—6.5 cm by 4.5 cm felt. Bloomer, Petticoat—40 cm by 9 cm white rayon. Skirt—25 cm by 10 cm lightweight cotton fabric. Dress, Bonnet—35 cm by 30 cm cotton print. Also—packing, cotton wadding, polyester batting.

FINISHED SIZE: Refer to diagram.

INSTRUCTIONS:

The basic method is the same as for Hiji, so refer to pages 50-64.

Put on shoes and stitch to fit each foot.

Make underwear, dress, and bonnet in same manner as for Mary.

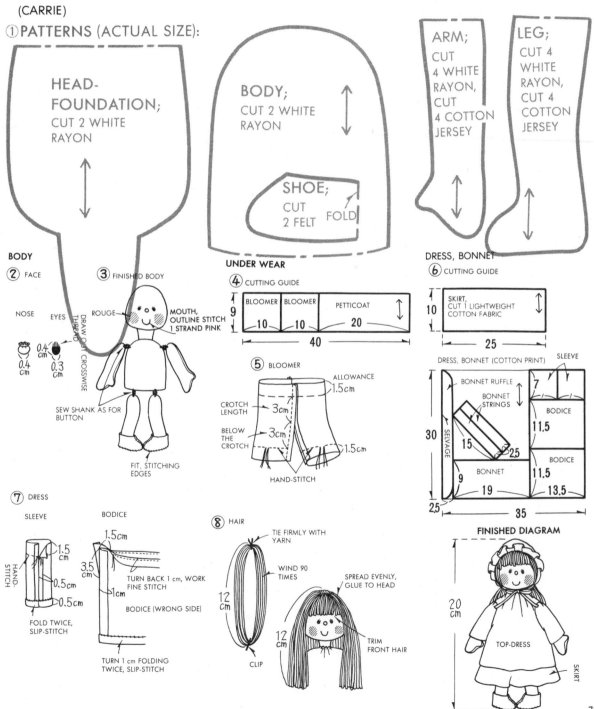

(CARRIE)

① PATTERNS (ACTUAL SIZE):

HEAD-FOUNDATION; CUT 2 WHITE RAYON

BODY; CUT 2 WHITE RAYON

SHOE; CUT 2 FELT FOLD

ARM; CUT 4 WHITE RAYON, CUT 4 COTTON JERSEY

LEG; CUT 4 WHITE RAYON, CUT 4 COTTON JERSEY

BODY
② FACE
③ FINISHED BODY

NOSE EYES DRAW OUT THREAD CROSSWISE ROUGE MOUTH, OUTLINE STITCH 1 STRAND PINK

0.4 cm 0.4 cm 0.3 cm

SEW SHANK AS FOR BUTTON

FIT, STITCHING EDGES

UNDER WEAR
④ CUTTING GUIDE

BLOOMER	BLOOMER	PETTICOAT
10	10	20

9

40

⑤ BLOOMER

ALLOWANCE 1.5cm
CROTCH LENGTH 3cm
BELOW THE CROTCH 3cm
1.5cm
HAND-STITCH

DRESS, BONNET
⑥ CUTTING GUIDE

SKIRT, CUT 1 LIGHTWEIGHT COTTON FABRIC

10   25

DRESS, BONNET (COTTON PRINT) SLEEVE

BONNET RUFFLE
BONNET STRINGS
SELVAGE
7
BODICE 11.5
BODICE 11.5 13.5
30   15 2.5
9 BONNET 19
25   35

⑦ DRESS

SLEEVE
HAND-STITCH
1.5 cm
0.5 cm
0.5 cm
FOLD TWICE, SLIP-STITCH

BODICE
1.5cm
3.5 cm
1cm
TURN BACK 1 cm, WORK FINE STITCH
BODICE (WRONG SIDE)
TURN 1 cm FOLDING TWICE, SLIP-STITCH

⑧ HAIR
TIE FIRMLY WITH YARN
WIND 90 TIMES
12 cm
12 cm
CLIP
SPREAD EVENLY, GLUE TO HEAD
TRIM FRONT HAIR

FINISHED DIAGRAM
20 cm
TOP-DRESS
SKIRT

LITTLE WOMEN

Shown on pages 6-7

These very pretty hug-dolls are as alike as four sisters should be. Use different print fabrics to make them. Because the hair longer length, use wool yarn if it is available.

YOU'LL NEED:
Head-Foundation, Body, Arms, Legs—55 cm by 45 cm white rayon. Face, Nose, Arms, Legs—70 cm by 38 cm cotton jersey. Eyes—dacron georgette. Mouth—strands of embroidery thread. Hair—bouclé. Dress, Bloomer, Ribbon—67 cm by 44 cm cotton print. Also—packing, cotton wadding, polyester batting.
FINISHED SIZE: Refer to diagram.

INSTRUCTIONS;
The basic method is the same as for Hiji, so refer to pages 50-64.
Sew bloomer, sleeves, and bodice on body in turn. Fasten the yarn for hair in the middle, secure at top of head. Apply glue, attach the yarn, parted on the side, and comb smooth. Put ribbon on head.

1 PATTERNS (ACTUAL SIZE):

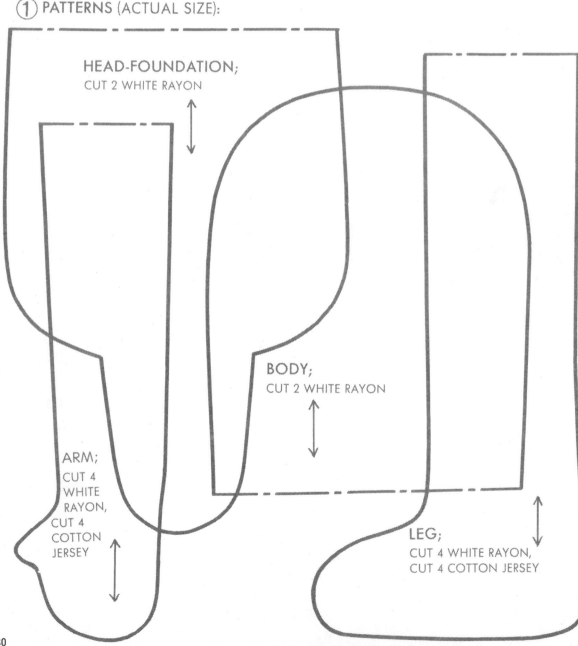

HEAD-FOUNDATION;
CUT 2 WHITE RAYON

BODY;
CUT 2 WHITE RAYON

ARM;
CUT 4 WHITE RAYON, CUT 4 COTTON JERSEY

LEG;
CUT 4 WHITE RAYON,
CUT 4 COTTON JERSEY

BODY

② FACE

NOSE
0.7cm

EYES
0.7 cm
0.5 cm

DRAW OUT CROSSWISE THREAD

③ FINISHED BODY

FRECKLES, USE BROWN FELT-TIP PEN

ROUGE

MOUTH, EMBROIDERY THREAD 6 STRANDS

SEW SHANK AS BUTTON

STUFF WITH POLYESTER BATTING

DRESS, BLOOMER, RIBBON

④ CUTTING GUIDE (COTTON PRINT)

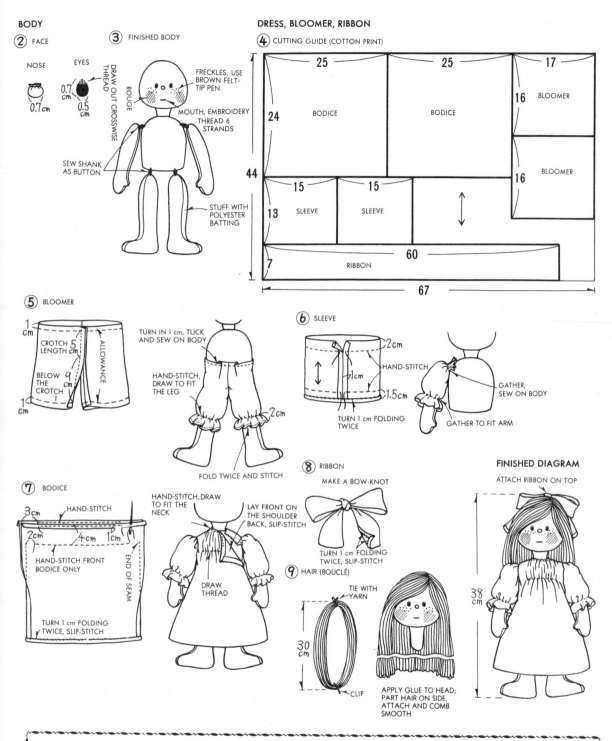

25 BODICE	25 BODICE	17
		16 BLOOMER
24		16 BLOOMER
44		
15 SLEEVE	15 SLEEVE	
13		
7 RIBBON	60	
67		

⑤ BLOOMER

1 cm
CROTCH LENGTH 5 cm
ALLOWANCE
BELOW THE CROTCH 9 cm
1 cm

TURN IN 1 cm, TUCK AND SEW ON BODY

HAND-STITCH, DRAW TO FIT THE LEG

2cm

FOLD TWICE AND STITCH

⑥ SLEEVE

2cm
HAND-STITCH
1cm
1.5cm
TURN 1 cm FOLDING TWICE

GATHER, SEW ON BODY
GATHER TO FIT ARM

FINISHED DIAGRAM

ATTACH RIBBON ON TOP

⑦ BODICE

3cm HAND-STITCH
2cm 4cm 1cm
END OF SEAM
HAND-STITCH FRONT BODICE ONLY
TURN 1 cm FOLDING TWICE, SLIP-STITCH

HAND-STITCH, DRAW TO FIT THE NECK

LAY FRONT ON THE SHOULDER BACK, SLIP-STITCH

DRAW THREAD

⑧ RIBBON

MAKE A BOW-KNOT

TURN 1 cm FOLDING TWICE, SLIP-STITCH

⑨ HAIR (BOUCLÉ)

TIE WITH YARN

30 cm

CLIP

APPLY GLUE TO HEAD; PART HAIR ON SIDE, ATTACH AND COMB SMOOTH

38 cm

MOTHER GOOSE

Shown on pages 8-9.

Bodies are simply made from scraps of fabric. Make individual dolls to suit the taste of each child.

(MONDAY'S CHILD)

YOU'LL NEED:

Head-Foundation—24 cm by 18 cm white rayon. Face, Nose—24 cm by 22 cm cotton jersey. Body, Arms, Skirt, Collar—21 cm by 75 cm velveteen, 110 cm of 1 cm lace.

Eyes—dacron georgette. Mouth—strands of embroidery thread. Hair—mohair yarn, 30 cm of 1 cm ribbon. Also—artificial flowers, packing, cotton wadding, polyester batting.

INSTRUCTIONS:

The basic method is the same as for Hiji, so refer to pages 50-64.

Make head-foundation and face as shown on pages 54-57.

Cut body, arms, skirt, and collar from velveteen.

Sew body leaving the opening for stuffing on back, stuff packing as firmly as possible into the top where neck is to be fixed. Then stuff polyester batting carefully beginning at toe.

Sew arm, make a slash on the inside, turn inside out and stuff with polyester batting.

Make a neck-size hole on the top of the body, apply glue, insert neck firmly into hole.

Attach hair following the steps shown on page 72.

*Use patterns below for all dolls, making head and body in this same manner.

① PATTERNS (ACTUAL SIZE):

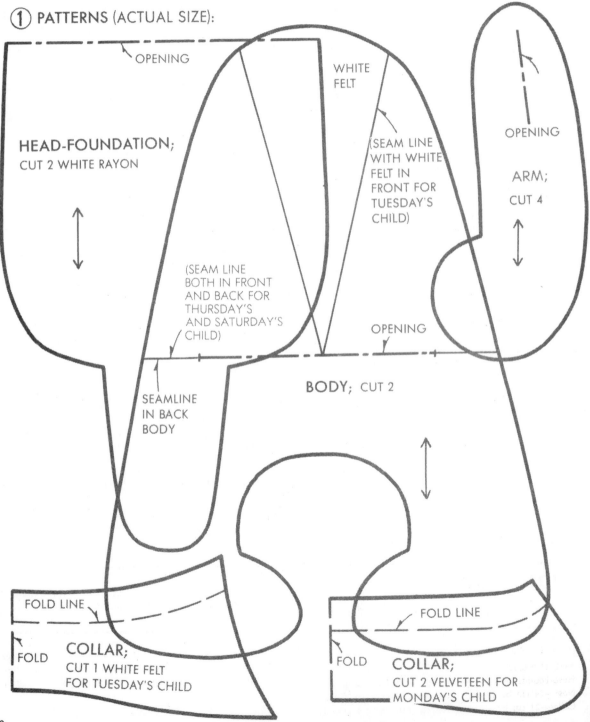

OPENING

HEAD-FOUNDATION;
CUT 2 WHITE RAYON

WHITE FELT

(SEAM LINE WITH WHITE FELT IN FRONT FOR TUESDAY'S CHILD)

OPENING

ARM;
CUT 4

(SEAM LINE BOTH IN FRONT AND BACK FOR THURSDAY'S AND SATURDAY'S CHILD)

OPENING

SEAMLINE IN BACK BODY

BODY; CUT 2

FOLD LINE

FOLD

COLLAR;
CUT 1 WHITE FELT FOR TUESDAY'S CHILD

FOLD LINE

FOLD

COLLAR;
CUT 2 VELVETEEN FOR MONDAY'S CHILD

BODY

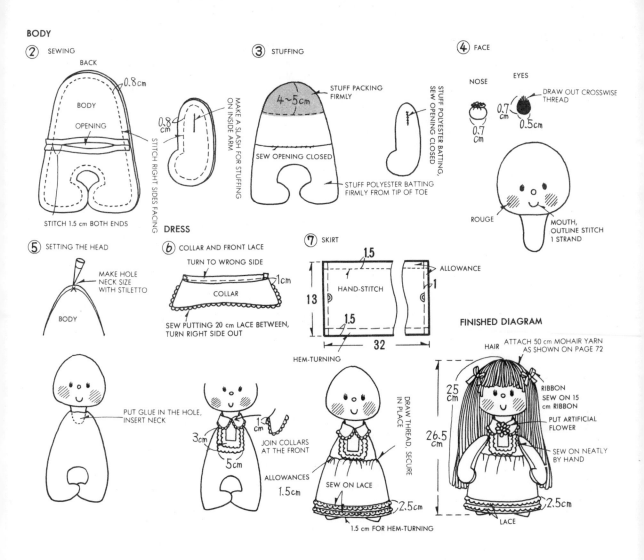

② SEWING

BACK

0.8cm

BODY
OPENING

0.8 cm

STITCH 1.5 cm BOTH ENDS

STITCH RIGHT SIDES FACING

MAKE A SLASH FOR STUFFING ON INSIDE ARM

③ STUFFING

STUFF PACKING FIRMLY

4~5cm

SEW OPENING CLOSED

STUFF POLYESTER BATTING FIRMLY FROM TIP OF TOE

STUFF POLYESTER BATTING, SEW OPENING CLOSED

④ FACE

NOSE   EYES

DRAW OUT CROSSWISE THREAD

0.7 cm   0.7 cm   0.5cm

ROUGE

MOUTH, OUTLINE STITCH 1 STRAND

DRESS

⑤ SETTING THE HEAD

MAKE HOLE NECK SIZE WITH STILETTO

BODY

PUT GLUE IN THE HOLE, INSERT NECK

⑥ COLLAR AND FRONT LACE

TURN TO WRONG SIDE

COLLAR

1cm

SEW PUTTING 20 cm LACE BETWEEN, TURN RIGHT SIDE OUT

3cm   1cm

5cm

JOIN COLLARS AT THE FRONT

ALLOWANCES 1.5 cm

⑦ SKIRT

1.5

13   HAND-STITCH

1.5

32

ALLOWANCE

1

HEM-TURNING

SEW ON LACE

DRAW THREAD, SECURE IN PLACE

2.5cm

1.5 cm FOR HEM-TURNING

FINISHED DIAGRAM

HAIR   ATTACH 50 cm MOHAIR YARN AS SHOWN ON PAGE 72

25 cm

26.5 cm

RIBBON SEW ON 15 cm RIBBON

PUT ARTIFICIAL FLOWER

SEW ON NEATLY BY HAND

2.5cm

LACE

(TUESDAY'S CHILD)
YOU'LL NEED:
Head-Foundation—24 cm by 18 cm white rayon. Face, Nose —24 cm by 22 cm cotton jersey. Body, Arms—42 cm by 24 cm velveteen. Eyes—dacron georgette. Mouth—strands of embroidery thread. Hair—mohair yarn. Collar, Yoke—20 cm by 10 cm felt. Also—6cm of 5 cm ribbon, packing, cotton wadding, polyester batting.

INSTRUCTIONS;
Make in same manner as Monday's child.
Make hair winding 2 strands of yarns around 2 fingers ten times, tie with white machine thread, secure to head as shown on page 67.

FINISHED DIAGRAM

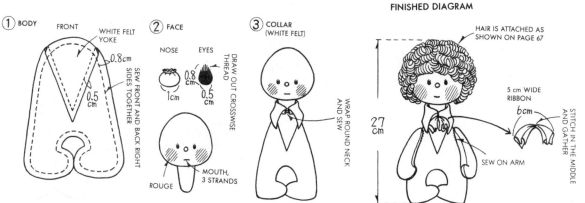

① BODY

FRONT

WHITE FELT YOKE

0.8cm

0.5 cm

SEW FRONT AND BACK RIGHT SIDES TOGETHER

② FACE

NOSE   EYES

DRAW OUT CROSSWISE THREAD

0.8 cm   0.5 cm

1cm

MOUTH, 3 STRANDS

ROUGE

③ COLLAR (WHITE FELT)

WRAP ROUND NECK AND SEW

HAIR IS ATTACHED AS SHOWN ON PAGE 67

27 cm

5 cm WIDE RIBBON

6cm

STITCH IN THE MIDDLE AND GATHER

SEW ON ARM

83

(WEDNESDAY'S CHILD)
YOU'LL NEED:

Head-Foundation—24 cm by 18 cm white rayon. Face, Nose—24 cm by 22 cm cotton jersey. Body, Arms, Skirt—72 cm by 24 cm velveteen. Eyes—dacron georgette. Mouth—strands of embroidery thread. Hair—mohair yarn. Apron, Cap—65 cm by 25 cm lightweight cotton fabric, 66 cm of 1.5 cm lace. Also—1.3 cm diameter button, 15 cm of 1.5 cm lace, packing, cotton wadding, polyester batting.

INSTRUCTIONS:

Make in same manner as Monday's child.
Make cap and apron.
Wrap lace round the neck, secure with button.

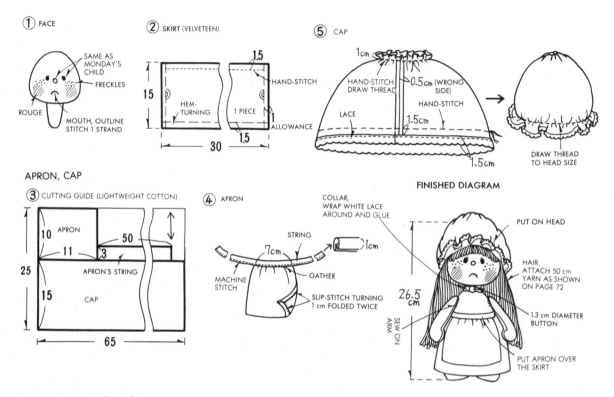

(THURSDAY'S CHILD)
YOU'LL NEED:

Head-Foundation—24 cm by 18 cm white rayon. Face, Nose—24 cm by 22 cm cotton jersey. Body, Arms—52 cm by 12 cm velveteen. Legs—30 cm by 11 cm corduroy. Eyes—dacron georgette. Mouth—strands of embroidery thread. Hair—mohair yarn. Scarf—15 cm by 15 cm wool. Cap, Suitcase—Heavyweight yarn. Also—3 of 0.8 cm diameter button, packing, cotton wadding, polyester batting.

INSTRUCTIONS;

Make in same manner as Monday's child.
Crochet cap with No. F crochet hook, and put on head.
Crochet suitcase with same yarn as cap.

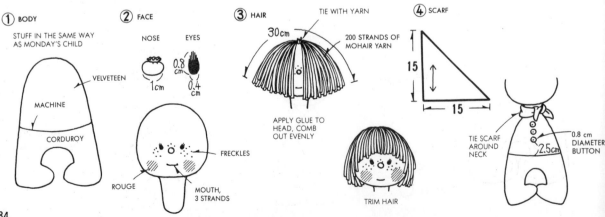

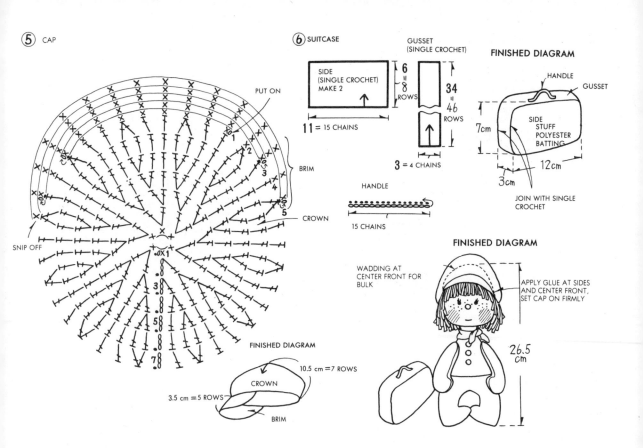

⑤ CAP

PUT ON

BRIM

CROWN

SNIP OFF

0 X 1

⑥ SUITCASE

SIDE
(SINGLE CROCHET)
MAKE 2

6 = 8 ROWS

11 = 15 CHAINS

GUSSET
(SINGLE CROCHET)

34 = 46 ROWS

3 = 4 CHAINS

HANDLE

15 CHAINS

FINISHED DIAGRAM

HANDLE

GUSSET

SIDE
STUFF
POLYESTER
BATTING

7cm

3cm

12cm

JOIN WITH SINGLE
CROCHET

FINISHED DIAGRAM

FINISHED DIAGRAM

10.5 cm = 7 ROWS

CROWN

3.5 cm = 5 ROWS

BRIM

WADDING AT
CENTER FRONT FOR
BULK

APPLY GLUE AT SIDES
AND CENTER FRONT,
SET CAP ON FIRMLY

26.5
cm

(FRIDAY'S CHILD)

YOU'LL NEED:
Head-Foundation—24 cm by 18 cm white rayon. Face, Nose—24 cm by 22 cm cotton jersey. Body, Skirt, Arms, Ribbon—80 cm by 19 cm velveten. Eyes—dacron georgette. Mouth—strands of embroidery thread. Hair—mohair yarn. Stole, Hair-Band—Lightweight yarn. Also—packing, cotton wadding, polyester bating.

INSTRUCTIONS:
Make in same manner as Monday's child. Crochet hair-band and stole with No. 4 hook.

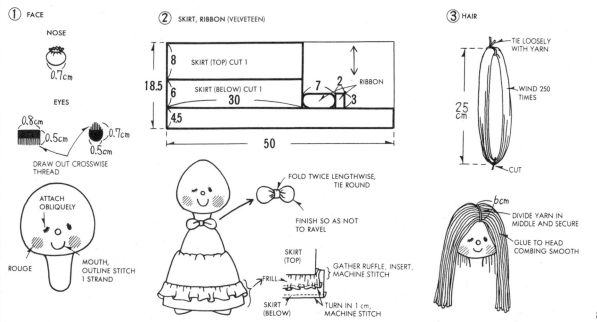

① FACE

NOSE

0.7cm

EYES

0.8cm
0.5cm
0.7cm
0.5cm

DRAW OUT CROSSWISE
THREAD

ATTACH
OBLIQUELY

ROUGE

MOUTH,
OUTLINE STITCH
1 STRAND

② SKIRT, RIBBON (VELVETEEN)

8 SKIRT (TOP) CUT 1

18.5

6 SKIRT (BELOW) CUT 1
30

4.5

50

7 2 RIBBON

3

FOLD TWICE LENGTHWISE,
TIE ROUND

FINISH SO AS NOT
TO RAVEL

SKIRT
(TOP)

FRILL

GATHER RUFFLE, INSERT,
MACHINE STITCH

SKIRT
(BELOW)

TURN IN 1 cm,
MACHINE STITCH

③ HAIR

TIE LOOSELY
WITH YARN

WIND 250
TIMES

25
cm

CUT

6cm

DIVIDE YARN IN
MIDDLE AND SECURE

GLUE TO HEAD
COMBING SMOOTH

85

④ STOLE (LIGHTWEIGHT YARN 1 STRAND)

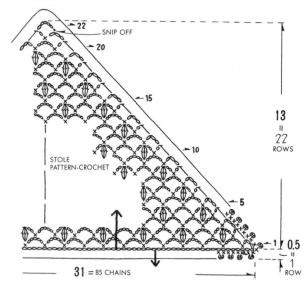

SNIP OFF

22

20

15

10

5

STOLE
PATTERN-CROCHET

13
=
22
ROWS

0.5
=
1
ROW

31 = 85 CHAINS

⑤ HAIR-BAND (LIGHTWEIGHT YARN 1 STRAND)

STRING, MAKE 2

16 = 50 CHAINS

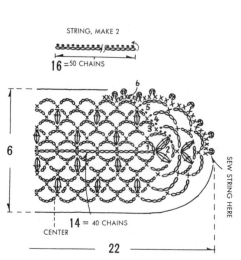

6

22

14 = 40 CHAINS

CENTER

SEW STRING HERE

FINISHED DIAGRAM

HAIR-BAND

HAIR,
25 cm LONG

LAY STOLE OVER THE
SHOULDER, SECURE THE
ENDS BELOW THE ARM

26.5
cm

(SATURDAY'S CHILD)

YOU'LL NEED:

Head-Foundation—24 cm by 18 cm white rayon. Face, Nose—24 cm by 22 cm cotton jersey. Body, Arms, Collar—52 cm by 20 cm velveteen. Legs —30 cm by 11 cm striped velveteen. Eyes—dacron georgette. Mouth— strands of embroidery thread. Hair—mohair yarn. Also—30 cm of 1 cm braid, 30 cm square gauze, packing, cotton wadding, polyester batting.

INSTRUCTIONS:

Cut out top and pants of body from different fabrics.

Make in same manner as Monday's child.

Sew hair of yarn all over head, without clipping.

① FACE

NOSE   EYES

0.5 cm

0.8cm   0.8cm

DRAW OUT CROSSWISE
THREAD

ATTACH
OBLIQUELY

FRECKLES

ROUGE

MOUTH,
OUTLINE STITCH
1 STRAND

② BODY

FRONT   BACK

GLUE BRAID

8
cm

22cm

LAP
1 cm

③ COLLAR (VELVETEEN)

8

1 PIECE

FOLD LINE

12

FOLD IN HALF RIGHT
SIDES FACING

SEW LEAVING 3 cm, TURN
RIGHT SIDE OUT

0.5 cm

MACHINE

2cm

0.5
cm

WRAP ROUND NECK
AND SECURE

FINISHED DIAGRAM

④ HAIR

WIND 2 STRANDS OF YARN
10 TIMES

TIE WITH
MACHINE THREAD

COVER HEAD WITH
YARN RINGLETS

FORM FOLLOWING RINGS WITHOUT
CUTTING YARN BETWEEN CURLS

⑤

30cm

PUT
WADDING

15cm

30cm

GAUZE

ROLL UP WITH
WADDING INSIDE

27
cm

SEW ON ARM

LAY OVER THE CHIN, TIE
AT TOP HEAD, APPLY GLUE

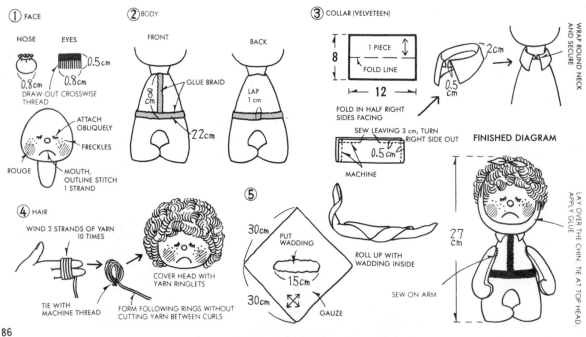
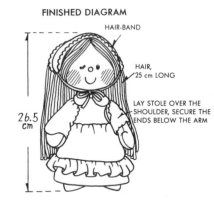

(SUNDAY'S CHILD)

YOU'LL NEED:

Head-Foundation—24 cm by 18 cm white rayon. Face, Nose—24 cm by 22 cm cotton jersey. Body, Arms, Skirt, Hood—75 cm by 26 cm velvetten. Eyes—dacron georgette. Mouth—strands of embroidery thread. Hair—mohair yarn. Apron—35 cm by 11 cm lightweight cotton fabric. Also—

100 cm of 1.5 cm lace, 10 cm of 0.5 cm ribbon, packing, cotton wadding, polyester batting.

INSTRUCTIONS:

Make in same manner as Monday's child. Sew on apron and attach hood.

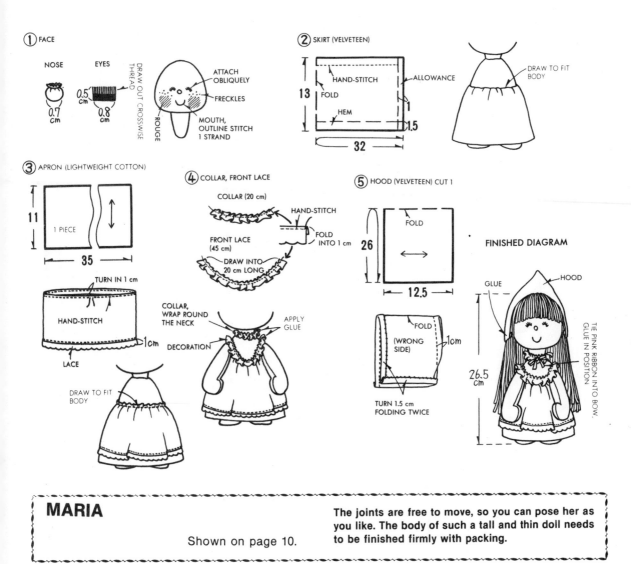

MARIA

Shown on page 10.

The joints are free to move, so you can pose her as you like. The body of such a tall and thin doll needs to be finished firmly with packing.

YOU'LL NEED:

Head-Foundation, Body, Arms, Legs—90 cm by 55 cm white rayon. Face, Nose, Arms—90 cm by 30 cm beige georgette. Legs—70 cm by 27 cm white georgette. Eyes—dacron georgette. Mounth—strands of embroidery thread. Hair—sport weitht yarn. Bloomer, Petticoat—85 cm by 34 cm broadcloth, 130 cm of 5 cm lace. Skirt—80 cm by 40 cm cotton print. Apron—28 cm by 35 cm crepe. Sleeves, Bodice—62 cm by 30 cm lace fabric, 80 cm of 3.5 cm lace. Vest—30 cm by 17 cm black felt, 40 cm of 1 cm tyrolean braid. Shoes—22 cm by 16 cm lightweight cotton fabric, 8 cm by 6 cm brown felt. Also—packing, cotton wadding, polyester

batting.

FINISHED SIZE: 74 cm tall.

INSTRUCTIONS

The basic method is the same as for Hiji, so refer to pages 50-64.

Make arms and legs that can be bent freely.

Cut fabric shoe pieces on bias and sew on.

Sew bodice front and back on neatly. Put vest on in same manner as bodice.

Make hair of yarn, glue on head and trim.

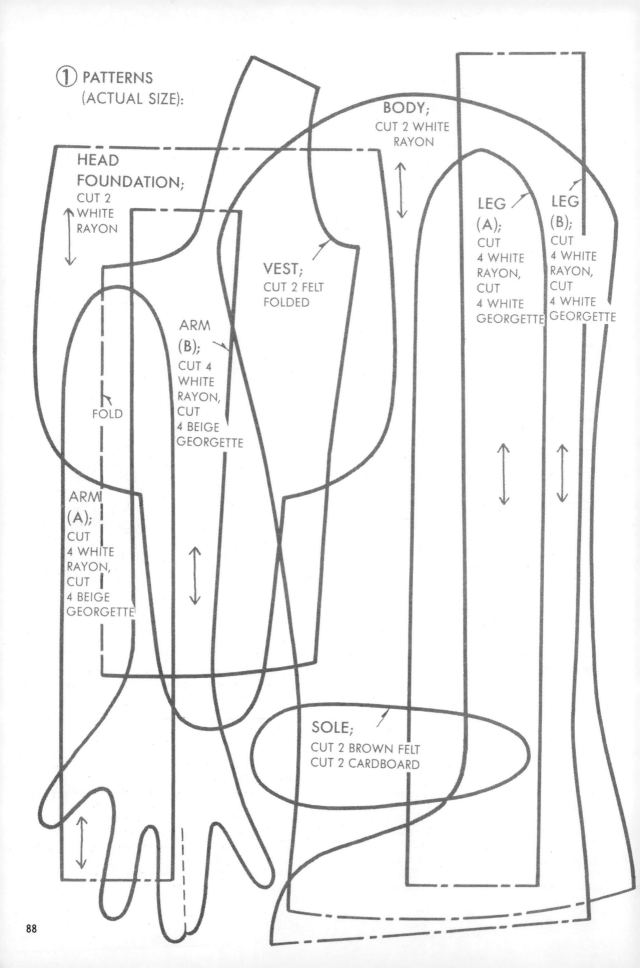

① PATTERNS
(ACTUAL SIZE):

BODY;
CUT 2 WHITE
RAYON

HEAD
FOUNDATION;
CUT 2
WHITE
RAYON

LEG
(A);
CUT
4 WHITE
RAYON,
CUT
4 WHITE
GEORGETTE

LEG
(B);
CUT
4 WHITE
RAYON,
CUT
4 WHITE
GEORGETTE

VEST;
CUT 2 FELT
FOLDED

ARM
(B);
CUT 4
WHITE
RAYON,
CUT
4 BEIGE
GEORGETTE

FOLD

ARM
(A);
CUT
4 WHITE
RAYON,
CUT
4 BEIGE
GEORGETTE

SOLE;
CUT 2 BROWN FELT
CUT 2 CARDBOARD

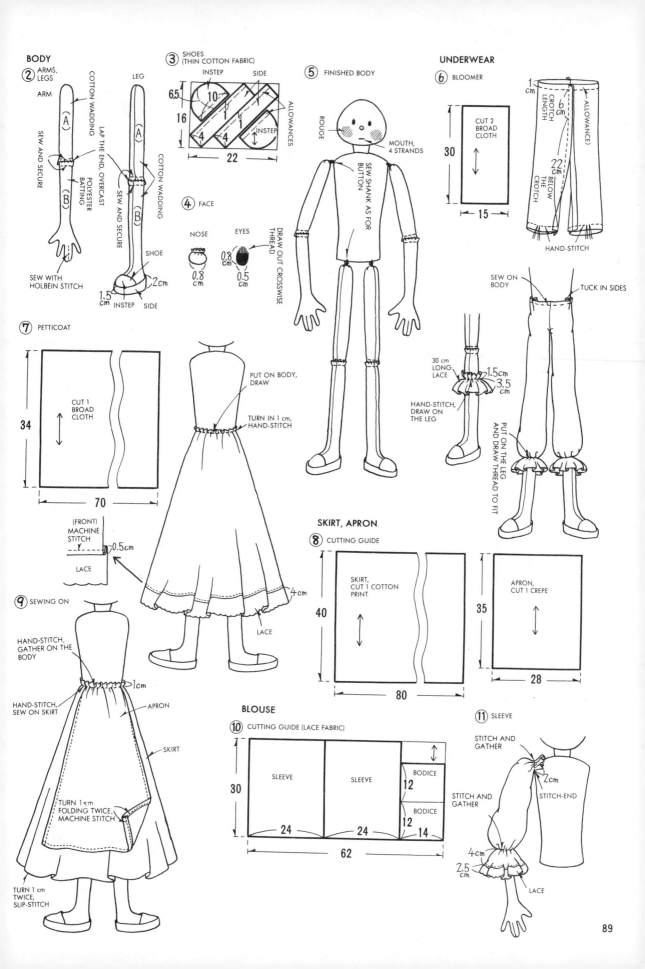

BODY

② ARMS, LEGS

ARM

COTTON WADDING

SEW AND SECURE

POLYESTER BATTING

(A)

(B)

SEW WITH HOLBEIN STITCH

LEG

COTTON WADDING

LAP THE END, OVERCAST

SEW AND SECURE

(A)

COTTON WADDING

(B)

SHOE

2cm

1.5cm INSTEP SIDE

③ SHOES (THIN COTTON FABRIC)

6.5

INSTEP

10

SIDE

16

4

1

1

INSTEP

INSTEP

ALLOWANCES

22

④ FACE

NOSE

0.8cm

EYES

0.8cm

0.5cm

DRAW OUT CROSSWISE THREAD

⑤ FINISHED BODY

ROUGE

MOUTH, 4 STRANDS

SEW SHANK AS FOR BUTTON

UNDERWEAR

⑥ BLOOMER

CUT 2 BROAD CLOTH

30

15

1cm

CROTCH LENGTH

6cm

ALLOWANCE)

22 BELOW THE CROTCH

HAND-STITCH

SEW ON BODY

TUCK IN SIDES

30 cm LONG LACE

1.5cm

3.5cm

HAND-STITCH, DRAW ON THE LEG

PUT ON THE LEG AND DRAW THREAD TO FIT

⑦ PETTICOAT

CUT 1 BROAD CLOTH

34

70

(FRONT) MACHINE STITCH

0.5cm

LACE

PUT ON BODY, DRAW

TURN IN 1 cm, HAND-STITCH

4cm

LACE

SKIRT, APRON

⑧ CUTTING GUIDE

SKIRT, CUT 1 COTTON PRINT

40

80

APRON, CUT 1 CREPE

35

28

⑨ SEWING ON

HAND-STITCH, GATHER ON THE BODY

HAND-STITCH, SEW ON SKIRT

1cm

APRON

SKIRT

TURN 1cm FOLDING TWICE, MACHINE STITCH

TURN 1 cm TWICE, SLIP-STITCH

BLOUSE

⑩ CUTTING GUIDE (LACE FABRIC)

30

SLEEVE

SLEEVE

24

24

BODICE

12

BODICE

12

14

62

⑪ SLEEVE

STITCH AND GATHER

2cm

STITCH-END

STITCH AND GATHER

4cm

2.5cm

LACE

89

12 COLLAR (30 cm LACE)

2.5cm
1cm
HAND-STITCH

2.5cm
WRAP ROUND NECK, GATHER

13 BODICE

SEW ON BODICE

FINISHED DIAGRAM

74 cm

TIE IN THE MIDDLE WITH YARN FIRMLY

GLUE TO HEAD COMB SMOOTH

VEST

14 FRONT BODICE

TURN IN 1 cm WRAPPING RAW EDGE

GLUE

TYROLEAN BRAID

0.3 cm

TURN IN 1 cm

15 CLOTHING

SLIP-STITCH SHOULDERS AND SIDES

16 HAIR

14cm

SECURE CENTER KNOT TO THE HEAD

ELIZA

Shown on page 11.

Use Maria's patterns. Try to image the town of London in winter. Make a carefree girl selling flowers at the market there.

YOU'LL NEED:

Head-Foundation, Body, Arms, Legs—90 cm by 55 cm white rayon. Face, Nose, Arms—90 cm by 30 cm beige georgette. Legs—70 cm by 27 cm black woolly nylon. Eyes—dacron georgette. Mouth—strands of embroidery thread. Hair—mohair yarn. Bloomer, Petticoat—85 cm by 34 cm broadcloth, 130 cm of 5 cm lace. Suit—92 cm by 56 cm velveteen. Blouse—46 cm by 34 cm crepe. Apron—80 cm by 40 cm cotton print. Scarf—23 cm by 23 cm georgette. Hat—black heavyweight yarn, 30 cm of 0.6 cm grosgrain ribbon, artificial flowers. Stole, Bag—frizzy yarn, Artificial flower. Shoes—18 cm by 13 cm corduroy. Also—packing, cotton wadding, polyester batting.

FINISHED, SIZE: Refer to diagram.
INSTRUCTIONS:

For the body, use Maria's pattern onpage 88, and make according to the basic instructions on pages 50-64.
Use black woolly nylon for leg fabric.
For the hair, make 80 cm long skein of yarn and sew on in same manner as Hiji, braid the yarn on sides.
Crochet hat, sew on a bunch of flowers.
Crochet stole with 1 strand, bag with 2 strands, and put a bunch of flowers inside the bag.

BODY

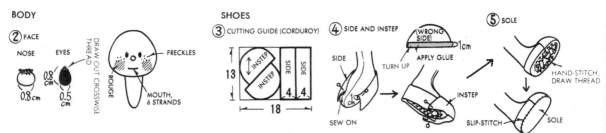

2 FACE

NOSE   EYES   FRECKLES

0.8 cm   0.8 cm   0.5 cm

DRAW OUT CROSSWISE THREAD

ROUGE

MOUTH, 6 STRANDS

SHOES

3 CUTTING GUIDE (CORDUROY)

INSTEP   INSTEP   SIDE   SIDE
13   4   4
18

4 SIDE AND INSTEP

SIDE   (WRONG SIDE)   1cm
TURN UP   APPLY GLUE
INSTEP
SEW ON

5 SOLE

HAND-STITCH, DRAW THREAD
SLIP-STITCH   SOLE

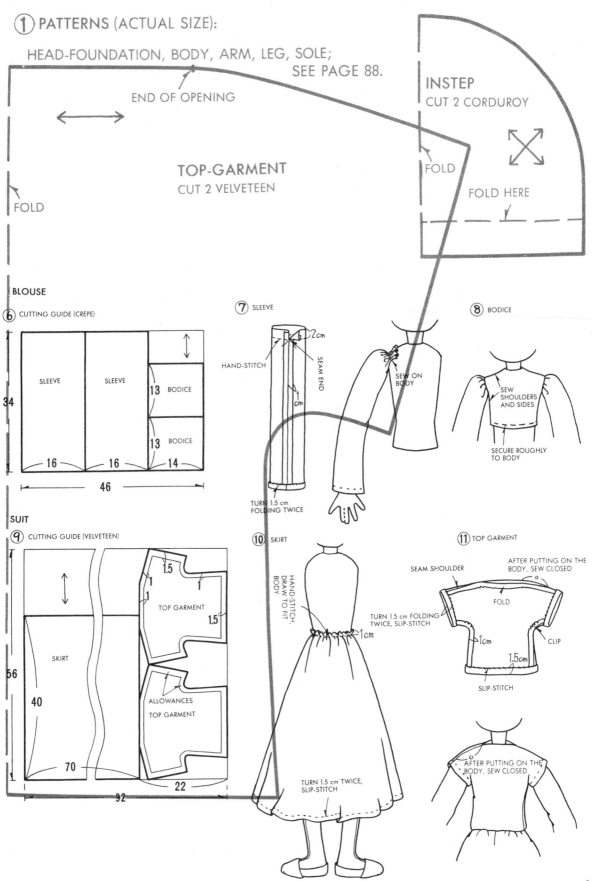

① PATTERNS (ACTUAL SIZE):

HEAD-FOUNDATION, BODY, ARM, LEG, SOLE;
SEE PAGE 88.

END OF OPENING

TOP-GARMENT
CUT 2 VELVETEEN

FOLD

INSTEP
CUT 2 CORDUROY

FOLD

FOLD HERE

BLOUSE

⑥ CUTTING GUIDE (CREPE)

34

SLEEVE   SLEEVE   13 BODICE

13 BODICE

16   16   14

46

⑦ SLEEVE

2 cm

HAND-STITCH

SEAM END

1 cm

TURN 1.5 cm
FOLDING TWICE

SEW ON
BODY

⑧ BODICE

SEW
SHOULDERS
AND SIDES

SECURE ROUGHLY
TO BODY

SUIT

⑨ CUTTING GUIDE (VELVETEEN)

1.5

1   1

TOP GARMENT

1.5

56   SKIRT

40

ALLOWANCES
TOP GARMENT

70

22

92

⑩ SKIRT

HAND-STITCH,
DRAW TO FIT
BODY

1cm

TURN 1.5 cm TWICE,
SLIP-STITCH

⑪ TOP GARMENT

SEAM SHOULDER

AFTER PUTTING ON THE
BODY, SEW CLOSED

FOLD

TURN 1.5 cm FOLDING
TWICE, SLIP-STITCH

1cm

CLIP

1.5cm

SLIP-STITCH

AFTER PUTTING ON THE
BODY, SEW CLOSED

APRON

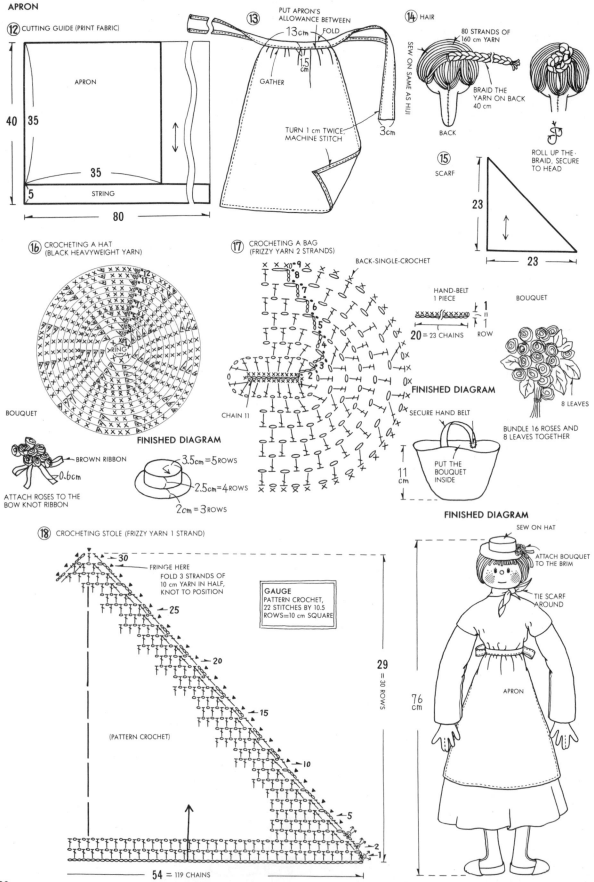

⑫ CUTTING GUIDE (PRINT FABRIC)

APRON

40   35

35

5   STRING

80

⑬ PUT APRON'S ALLOWANCE BETWEEN FOLD
13cm
1.5cm
GATHER
TURN 1 cm TWICE; MACHINE STITCH
3cm

⑭ HAIR
80 STRANDS OF 160 cm YARN
SEW ON SAME AS HIJI
BRAID THE YARN ON BACK 40 cm
BACK
ROLL UP THE BRAID, SECURE TO HEAD

⑮ SCARF
23
23

⑯ CROCHETING A HAT (BLACK HEAVYWEIGHT YARN)
RING
BOUQUET
ATTACH ROSES TO THE BOW KNOT RIBBON
BROWN RIBBON
0.6cm

FINISHED DIAGRAM
3.5cm = 5 ROWS
2.5cm = 4 ROWS
2cm = 3 ROWS

⑰ CROCHETING A BAG (FRIZZY YARN 2 STRANDS)
BACK-SINGLE-CROCHET
CHAIN 11

HAND-BELT 1 PIECE
20 = 23 CHAINS
1 ROW

BOUQUET
8 LEAVES
BUNDLE 16 ROSES AND 8 LEAVES TOGETHER

FINISHED DIAGRAM
SECURE HAND BELT
11 cm
PUT THE BOUQUET INSIDE

FINISHED DIAGRAM

⑱ CROCHETING STOLE (FRIZZY YARN 1 STRAND)
30
FRINGE HERE
FOLD 3 STRANDS OF 10 cm YARN IN HALF, KNOT TO POSITION
25
20
15
10
5
2
1
(PATTERN CROCHET)
54 = 119 CHAINS

GAUGE
PATTERN CROCHET, 22 STITCHES BY 10.5 ROWS = 10 cm SQUARE

29 = 30 ROWS

SEW ON HAT
ATTACH BOUQUET TO THE BRIM
TIE SCARF AROUND
APRON
76 cm

92

ROSALIE

Shown on page 12.

This is a hug-doll like Hiji and easily made. Use colored tatting thread as hair, clipping skeins in the middle.

YOU'LL NEED:

Head-Foundation, Body, Arms, Legs—50 cm by 30 cm white rayon. Face, Nose, Arms, Legs—40 cm by 27 cm beige georgette. Eyes—dacron georgette. Mouth—strands of embroidery thread. Hair—3 skeins of pink tatting thread, 50 cm of 0.5 cm ribbon. Bloomer, Petticoat—65 cm by 14 cm broadcloth, 35 cm of 1.8 cm lace. Skirt, Bodice—45 cm by 60 cm cotton print. Sleeves, Apron—52 cm by 12 cm lawn, 10 cm of 2.5 cm lace. Also—packing, cotton wadding, polyester batting.

FINISHED SIZE: Refer to diagram.
INSTRUCTIONS:

The basic method is the same as for Hiji, so refer to pages 50-64.

Stuff legs with polyester batting and finish in the same way as arms.

Attach hair as shown on page 72.

Use selvage side for the skirt ruffle, but if not available, finish cut edges by folding twice.

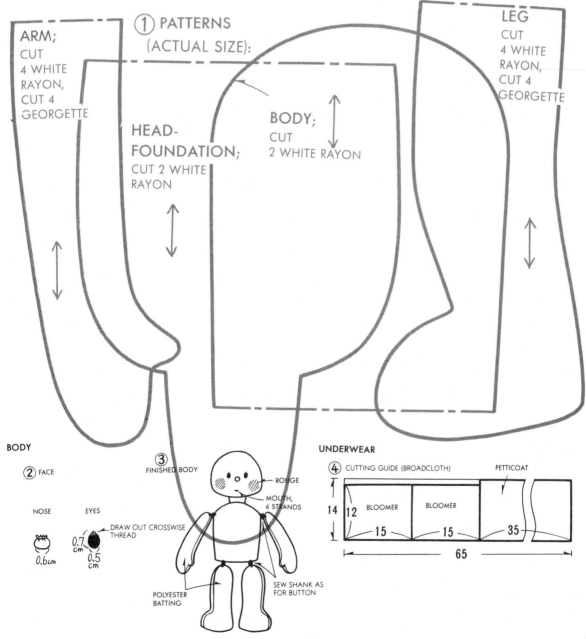

① PATTERNS (ACTUAL SIZE):

ARM; CUT 4 WHITE RAYON, CUT 4 GEORGETTE

HEAD-FOUNDATION; CUT 2 WHITE RAYON

BODY; CUT 2 WHITE RAYON

LEG CUT 4 WHITE RAYON, CUT 4 GEORGETTE

BODY

② FACE

NOSE — 0.6cm

EYES — 0.7 cm, 0.5 cm — DRAW OUT CROSSWISE THREAD

③ FINISHED BODY

ROUGE

MOUTH, 6 STRANDS

POLYESTER BATTING

SEW SHANK AS FOR BUTTON

UNDERWEAR

④ CUTTING GUIDE (BROADCLOTH)

PETTICOAT

	12	BLOOMER	BLOOMER	
14		15	15	35

65

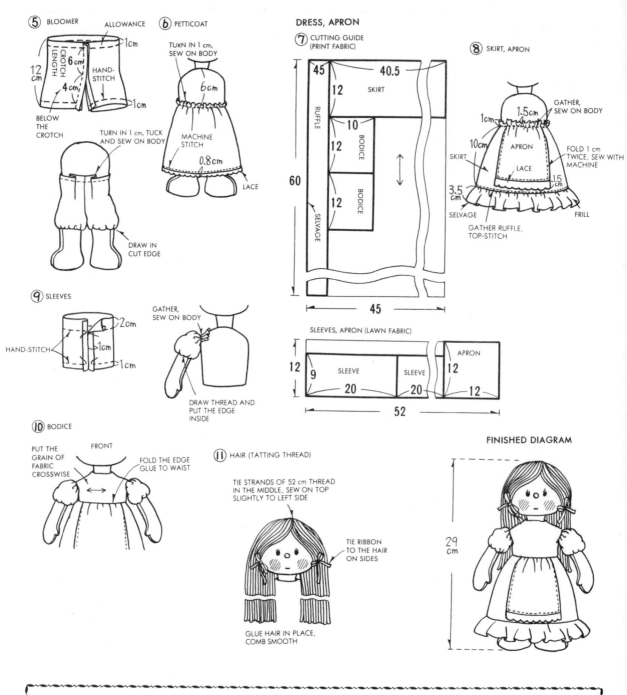

⑤ BLOOMER

ALLOWANCE
1cm
CROTCH LENGTH
12 cm
6 cm
HAND-STITCH
4 cm
1cm
BELOW THE CROTCH
TURN IN 1 cm, TUCK AND SEW ON BODY
DRAW IN CUT EDGE

⑥ PETTICOAT

TURN IN 1 cm, SEW ON BODY
6cm
MACHINE STITCH
0.8cm
LACE

DRESS, APRON

⑦ CUTTING GUIDE (PRINT FABRIC)

45	40.5
RUFFLE
12 — SKIRT
10
12 — BODICE
60
12 — BODICE
SELVAGE
45

⑧ SKIRT, APRON

GATHER, SEW ON BODY
1cm
1.5cm
10cm
APRON
SKIRT
LACE
3.5 cm
SELVAGE
1.5
FOLD 1 cm TWICE, SEW WITH MACHINE
FRILL
GATHER RUFFLE, TOP-STITCH

⑨ SLEEVES

2cm
1cm
HAND-STITCH
1cm
GATHER, SEW ON BODY
DRAW THREAD AND PUT THE EDGE INSIDE

SLEEVES, APRON (LAWN FABRIC)

12	9	SLEEVE	SLEEVE	APRON 12
	20		20	12
52

⑩ BODICE

PUT THE GRAIN OF FABRIC CROSSWISE
FRONT
FOLD THE EDGE GLUE TO WAIST

⑪ HAIR (TATTING THREAD)

TIE STRANDS OF 52 cm THREAD IN THE MIDDLE, SEW ON TOP SLIGHTLY TO LEFT SIDE
TIE RIBBON TO THE HAIR ON SIDES
GLUE HAIR IN PLACE, COMB SMOOTH

FINISHED DIAGRAM

29 cm

ELLEN

Shown on page 13.

This doll, with hair that is taffy colored, is ready to go to sleep in her nightgown, so use a soft pastel fabric to express this quiet time of day.

YOU'LL NEED:

Head-Foundation, Body, Arms, Legs—70 cm by 45 cm white rayon. Face, Nose, Arms, Legs—60 cm by 30 cm beige georgette. Eyes—dacron georgette. Mouth—strands of embroidery thread. Hair—3 skeins of tatting thread. Nightcap, Nightgown, Bloomer—90 cm by 70 cm cotton print, 340 cm of 2.5 cm lace, 35 cm of 0.5 cm ribbon. Slipper—30 cm by 12 cm felt. Also—packing, cotton wadding, polyester batting.

FINISHED SIZE: Refer to diagram.

INSTRUCTIONS:

The basic method is the same as for Hiji, so refer to pages 50-64.

Make feet, putting cardboard in soles in same manner as for Hiji, sew on instep and soles of slipper. Put on nightgown after the skirt is stitched to the body. Sew on hair as shown on page 72, set on nightcap.

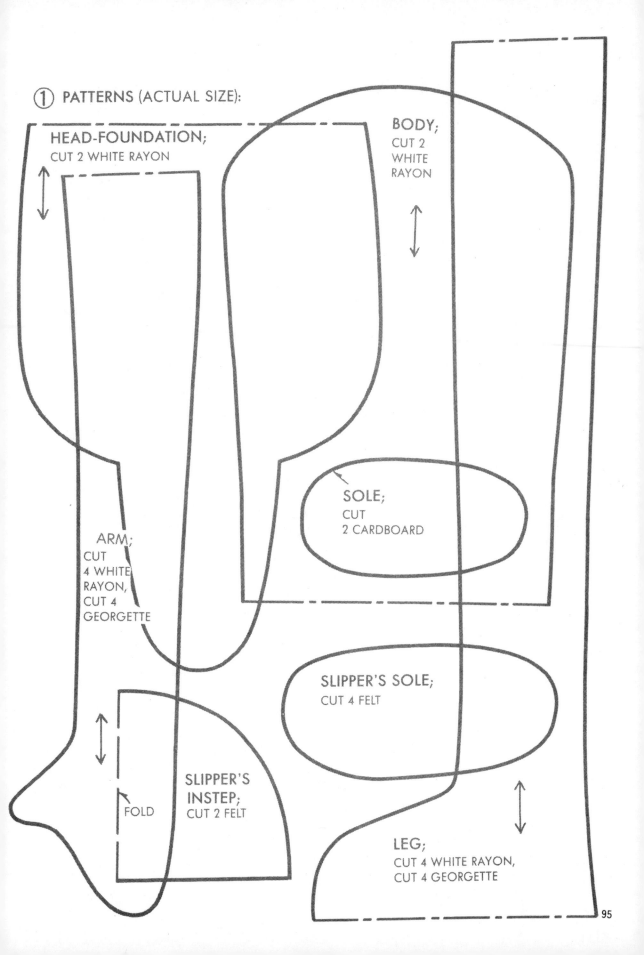

① PATTERNS (ACTUAL SIZE):

HEAD-FOUNDATION;
CUT 2 WHITE RAYON

BODY;
CUT 2
WHITE
RAYON

SOLE;
CUT
2 CARDBOARD

ARM;
CUT
4 WHITE
RAYON,
CUT 4
GEORGETTE

SLIPPER'S SOLE;
CUT 4 FELT

SLIPPER'S
INSTEP;
CUT 2 FELT

FOLD

LEG;
CUT 4 WHITE RAYON,
CUT 4 GEORGETTE

95

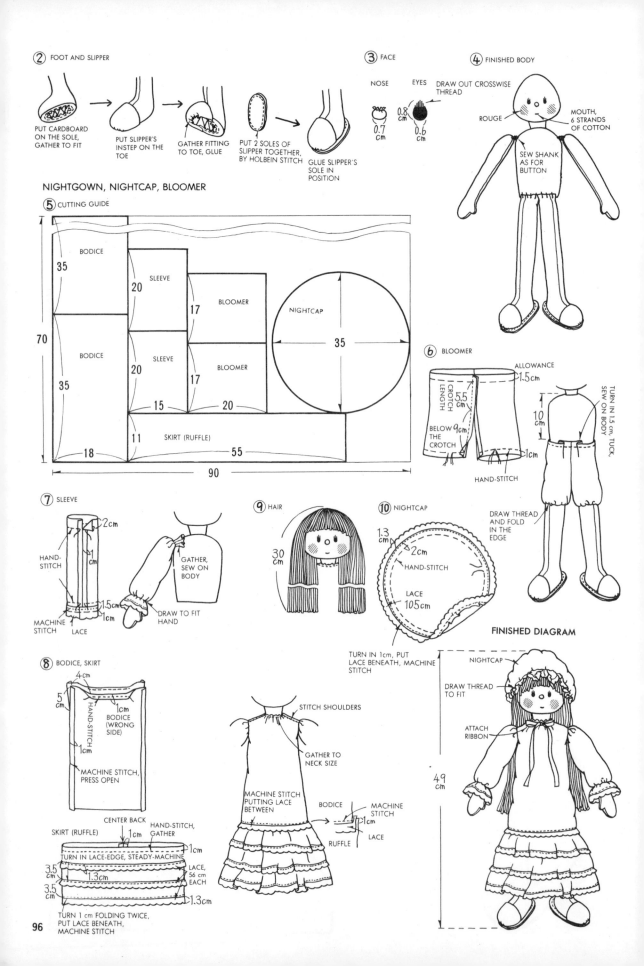

② FOOT AND SLIPPER

PUT CARDBOARD ON THE SOLE, GATHER TO FIT

PUT SLIPPER'S INSTEP ON THE TOE

GATHER FITTING TO TOE, GLUE

PUT 2 SOLES OF SLIPPER TOGETHER, BY HOLBEIN STITCH

GLUE SLIPPER'S SOLE IN POSITION

③ FACE

NOSE 0.7 cm

EYES 0.8 cm / 0.6 cm

④ FINISHED BODY

DRAW OUT CROSSWISE THREAD

ROUGE

MOUTH, 6 STRANDS OF COTTON

SEW SHANK AS FOR BUTTON

NIGHTGOWN, NIGHTCAP, BLOOMER

⑤ CUTTING GUIDE

BODICE 35
BODICE 35
70
18
SLEEVE 20
SLEEVE 20
15
11
BLOOMER 17
BLOOMER 17
20
SKIRT (RUFFLE)
NIGHTCAP 35
55
90

⑥ BLOOMER

ALLOWANCE 1.5cm

CROTCH LENGTH 5.5
BELOW 9cm THE CROTCH
1cm

HAND-STITCH

10 cm

TURN IN 1.5 cm, TUCK, SEW ON BODY

DRAW THREAD AND FOLD IN THE EDGE

⑦ SLEEVE

2cm
1 cm
HAND-STITCH
1.5cm
1cm
MACHINE STITCH
LACE

GATHER, SEW ON BODY

DRAW TO FIT HAND

⑨ HAIR

30 cm

⑩ NIGHTCAP

1.3 cm
2cm
HAND-STITCH
LACE 105cm

TURN IN 1cm, PUT LACE BENEATH, MACHINE STITCH

FINISHED DIAGRAM

⑧ BODICE, SKIRT

4cm
5 cm
HAND-STITCH
1cm
BODICE (WRONG SIDE)
1cm
MACHINE STITCH, PRESS OPEN

STITCH SHOULDERS

GATHER TO NECK SIZE

MACHINE STITCH PUTTING LACE BETWEEN

BODICE
MACHINE STITCH
1cm
RUFFLE
LACE

SKIRT (RUFFLE)
CENTER BACK
HAND-STITCH, GATHER
1cm
1cm
TURN IN LACE-EDGE, STEADY-MACHINE
3.5 cm
1.3cm
LACE, 56 cm EACH
3.5 cm
1.3cm
TURN 1 cm FOLDING TWICE, PUT LACE BENEATH, MACHINE STITCH

NIGHTCAP

DRAW THREAD TO FIT

ATTACH RIBBON

49 cm

96

MAYU

Shown on page 14.

Shown on page 14.

Use new-born baby socks instead of shoes, and since the top of the arms and legs have to be stuffed thicker than the opening, use polyester batting instead of wadding.

YOU'LL NEED:
Head-Foundation, Body, Arms, Legs—90 cm by 65 cm white rayon. Face, Nose, Arms—dacron georgette. Mouth—strands of embroidery thread. Hair—sport-weight yarn, 60 cm of 0.6 cm ribbon Bloomer, Dress—90 cm by 30 cm cotton print, 18 cm by 14 cm broadcloth, 70 cm of 3 cm lace, 1.5 cm diameter button. Also—new-born baby socks, packing, cotton wadding, polyester batting

FINISHED SIZE: Refer to diagram.
INSTRUCTIONS;
The basic method is the same as for Hiji, so refer to pages 50-64.
Legs are finished in the same way as arms, by stuffing with polyster batting. Sew on front bodice after lace is stitched to the yoke.
Sew on hair same as Hiji's braid the sides, loop the braids and secure with ribbons.

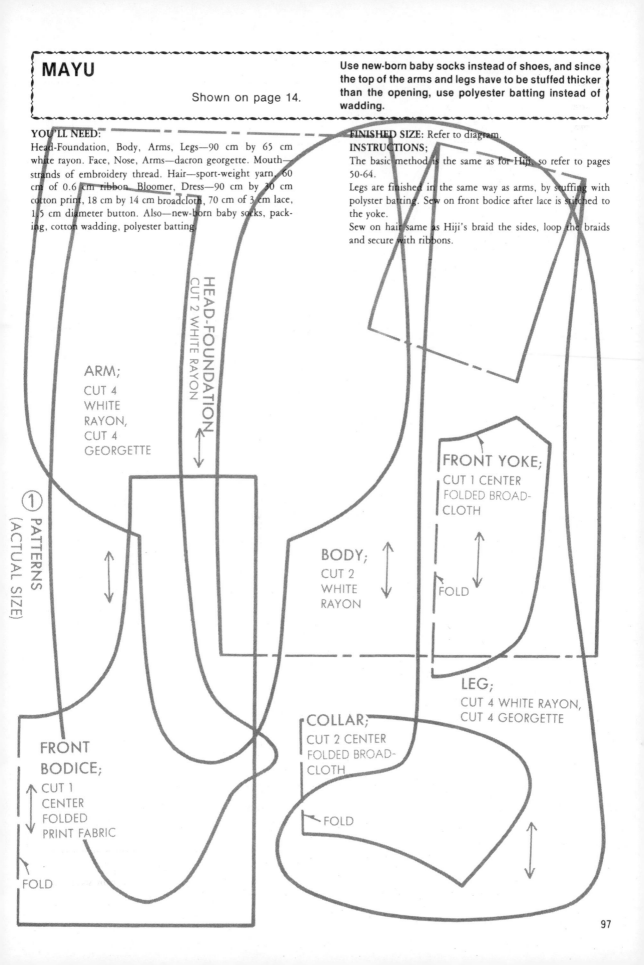

① PATTERNS (ACTUAL SIZE)

HEAD-FOUNDATION
CUT 2 WHITE RAYON

ARM;
CUT 4 WHITE RAYON,
CUT 4 GEORGETTE

BODY;
CUT 2 WHITE RAYON

FRONT YOKE;
CUT 1 CENTER FOLDED BROAD-CLOTH

FOLD

LEG;
CUT 4 WHITE RAYON,
CUT 4 GEORGETTE

FRONT BODICE;
CUT 1 CENTER FOLDED PRINT FABRIC

FOLD

COLLAR;
CUT 2 CENTER FOLDED BROAD-CLOTH

FOLD

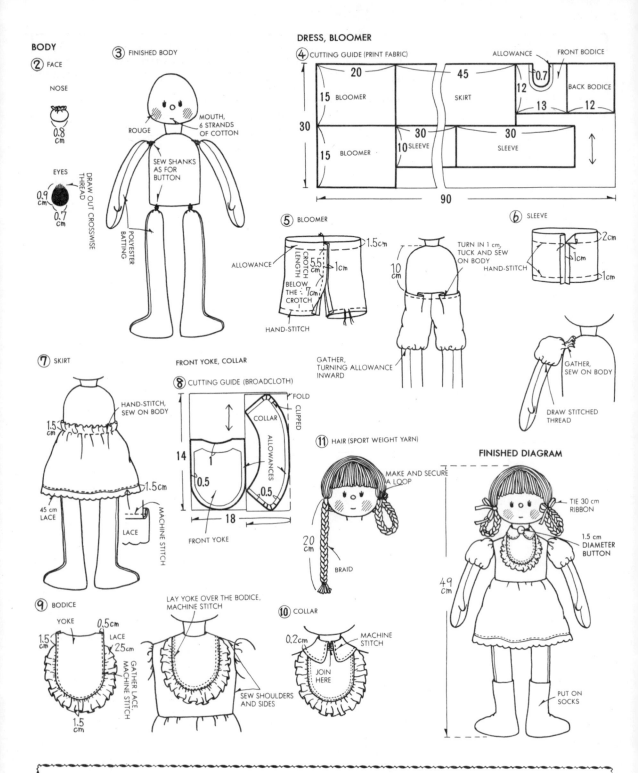

BODY

② FACE

NOSE

0.8 cm

EYES

0.9 cm

0.7 cm

DRAW OUT CROSSWISE THREAD

③ FINISHED BODY

MOUTH, 6 STRANDS OF COTTON

ROUGE

SEW SHANKS AS FOR BUTTON

POLYESTER BATTING

DRESS, BLOOMER

④ CUTTING GUIDE (PRINT FABRIC)

ALLOWANCE

FRONT BODICE

20

BLOOMER   15

45

SKIRT

0.7

12

BACK BODICE

13   12

30

BLOOMER   15

30

10 SLEEVE

30

SLEEVE

90

⑤ BLOOMER

ALLOWANCE

CROTCH LENGTH

1.5cm

5.5 cm   1cm

BELOW THE CROTCH   7cm

HAND-STITCH

TURN IN 1 cm, TUCK AND SEW ON BODY
HAND-STITCH

10 cm

GATHER, TURNING ALLOWANCE INWARD

⑥ SLEEVE

2cm

1cm

1cm

GATHER, SEW ON BODY

DRAW STITCHED THREAD

⑦ SKIRT

1.5 cm

HAND-STITCH, SEW ON BODY

1.5 cm

45 cm LACE

LACE

MACHINE STITCH

⑧ CUTTING GUIDE (BROADCLOTH)

FOLD

CLIPPED

COLLAR

ALLOWANCES

14

1

0.5

0.5

18

FRONT YOKE

⑪ HAIR (SPORT WEIGHT YARN)

MAKE AND SECURE A LOOP

20 cm

BRAID

FINISHED DIAGRAM

TIE 30 cm RIBBON

1.5 cm DIAMETER BUTTON

49 cm

PUT ON SOCKS

⑨ BODICE

YOKE

0.5cm

1.5 cm

LACE 25cm

GATHER LACE, MACHINE STITCH

1.5 cm

LAY YOKE OVER THE BODICE, MACHINE STITCH

SEW SHOULDERS AND SIDES

⑩ COLLAR

0.2cm

MACHINE STITCH

JOIN HERE

SHIGERU & CHIKO

Shown on page 15.

Use new-born baby socks. Sweater and muffler are paired like those of a modern young couple.

YOU'LL NEED (body materials are for both):
Head-Foundation, Body, Arms, Legs—73 cm by 48 cm white rayon. Face, Nose, Arms, Legs—63 cm by 48 cm beige cotton jersey. Eyes—dacron georgette. Mouth—

strands of embroidery thread. Hair—sport-weight yarn, 40 cm of 0.6 cm ribbon. Also—New-born baby socks, packing, cotton wadding, polyester batting.

(Shigeru): Sweater—lighweight yarn. Pants—36 cm by 12 cm wool fabric.

(Chiko): Blouse—70 cm by 16 cm white jersey, 23 cm of 1 cm braid. Bloomer—36 cm by 12 cm white rayon. Jumper Skirt—20 cm by 23.5 cm felt, strands of embroidery cotton, Two 1.5 cm diameter buttons.

FINISHED SIZE: Refer to diagram.

INSTRUCTIONS;

The basic method is the same as for Hiji, so refer to pages 50-64.

(Shigeru): Make head beforehand, and set in position by making a hole on the body after sweater is on. Sew on hair as shown on page 72.

(Chiko): Make the body in same way as for Shigeru. Part the yarn for hair in half, sew on in same manner as Hiji's, as shown. Knit muffler, wrap round the neck.

① PATTERNS (ACTUAL SIZE):

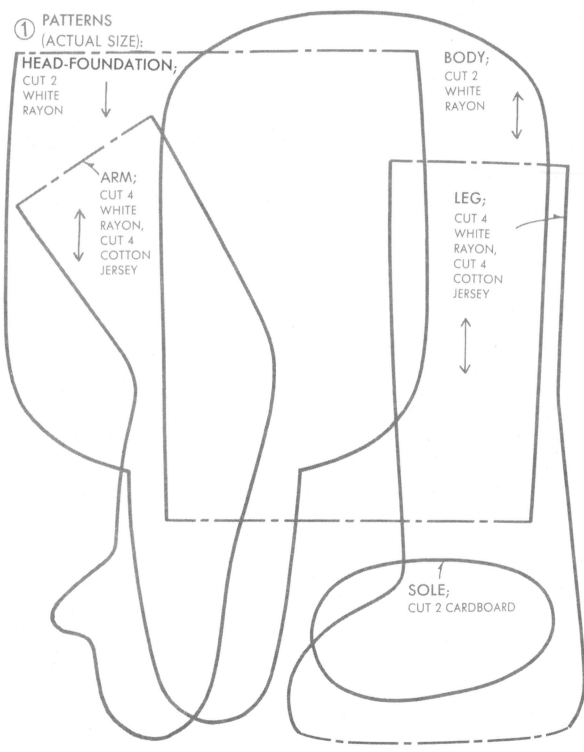

HEAD-FOUNDATION;
CUT 2
WHITE
RAYON

BODY;
CUT 2
WHITE
RAYON

ARM;
CUT 4
WHITE
RAYON,
CUT 4
COTTON
JERSEY

LEG;
CUT 4
WHITE
RAYON,
CUT 4
COTTON
JERSEY

SOLE;
CUT 2 CARDBOARD

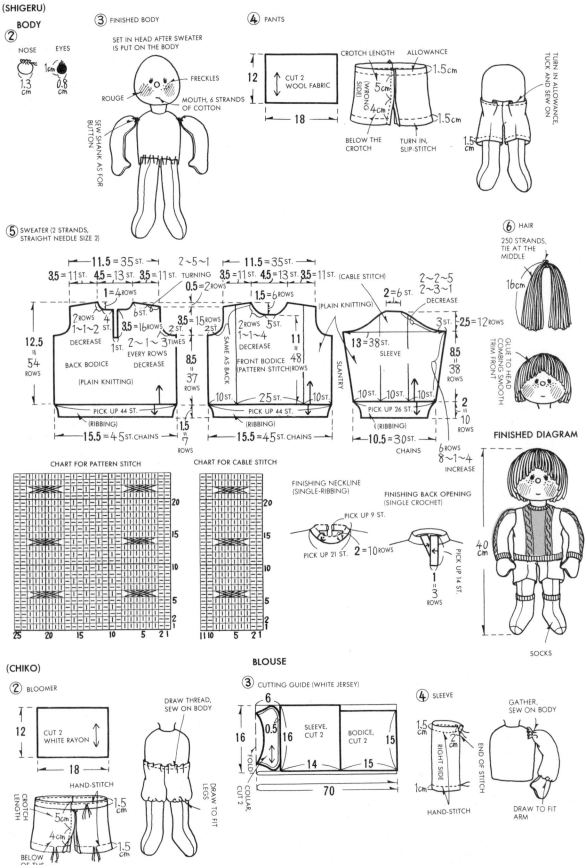

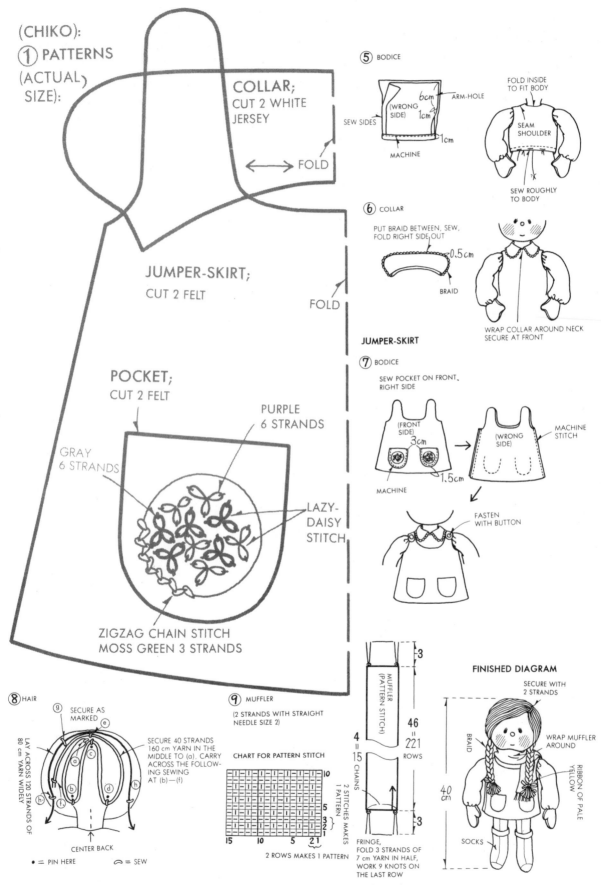

(CHIKO):
① PATTERNS
(ACTUAL
SIZE):

COLLAR;
CUT 2 WHITE
JERSEY

← FOLD →

FOLD

JUMPER-SKIRT;
CUT 2 FELT

FOLD

POCKET;
CUT 2 FELT

PURPLE
6 STRANDS

GRAY
6 STRANDS

LAZY-
DAISY
STITCH

ZIGZAG CHAIN STITCH
MOSS GREEN 3 STRANDS

⑤ BODICE

6cm
(WRONG SIDE) 1cm
SEW SIDES
1cm
MACHINE
ARM-HOLE

FOLD INSIDE
TO FIT BODY

SEAM
SHOULDER

SEW ROUGHLY
TO BODY

⑥ COLLAR

PUT BRAID BETWEEN, SEW,
FOLD RIGHT SIDE OUT
0.5cm
BRAID

WRAP COLLAR AROUND NECK
SECURE AT FRONT

JUMPER-SKIRT

⑦ BODICE

SEW POCKET ON FRONT,
RIGHT SIDE

(FRONT SIDE)
3cm
1.5cm
MACHINE

(WRONG SIDE)
MACHINE STITCH

FASTEN
WITH BUTTON

⑧ HAIR

SECURE AS
MARKED

g
e
c
a
b
f
d
h

LAY ACROSS 120 STRANDS OF 80 cm YARN WIDELY

SECURE 40 STRANDS
160 cm YARN IN THE
MIDDLE TO (a), CARRY
ACROSS THE FOLLOW-
ING SEWING
AT (b)—(f)

CENTER BACK

● = PIN HERE   ⌒ = SEW

⑨ MUFFLER

(2 STRANDS WITH STRAIGHT
NEEDLE SIZE 2)

CHART FOR PATTERN STITCH

15 10 5 2 1

10

5
3
2
1

2 STITCHES MAKES
1 PATTERN

2 ROWS MAKES 1 PATTERN

MUFFLER
(PATTERN STITCH)

3

46
=
221
ROWS

4
=
15
CHAINS

3

FRINGE,
FOLD 3 STRANDS OF
7 cm YARN IN HALF,
WORK 9 KNOTS ON
THE LAST ROW

FINISHED DIAGRAM

SECURE WITH
2 STRANDS

BRAID

WRAP MUFFLER
AROUND

RIBBON OF PALE
YELLOW

40 cm

SOCKS

AKKO & GORO & KENTA

Shown on pages 16–17.

Stain their clothes with gray powder eye-shadow. The three are from one pattern, and the boys clothes are made the same way. These playmates with mischievous faces have been in the dirt!

YOU'LL NEED (body materials are for the set):
Head-Foundation, Body, Arms, Legs—70 cm by 38 cm white rayon. Face, Nose, Arms, Legs—55 cm by 25 cm cotton jersey. Eyes—dacron georgette. Mouth—strands of embroidery thread. Hair—lightweight yarn, 40 cm of 0.6 cm ribbon. Also—packing, cotton wadding, polyester batting.
(Akko): Dress, Bloomer—58 cm by 29 cm cotton print. Adhesive plaster—white cotton fabric.
(Goro): Shirt—50 cm by 14 cm cotton print. Overalls—56 cm by 18 cm lightweight denim, strands of embroidery cotton.

(Kenta): Shirt—50 cm by 14 cm striped cotton. Overalls—56 cm by 18 cm lightweight denim, strands of embroidery cotton.
FINISHED SIZE: Refer to diagram.
INSTRUCTIONS:
Make three bodies in the same way, referring to pages 50-64 for basic directions.
Akk: Cut out dress and bloomers as shown and put on body. Sew on hair in same manner as for Hiji, making a braid and ribbon loop on each side.
Goro: Cut out shirt and overall as shown and put on body. Sew on hair (refer to page 72).
Kenta: Make in same manner as for Goro.

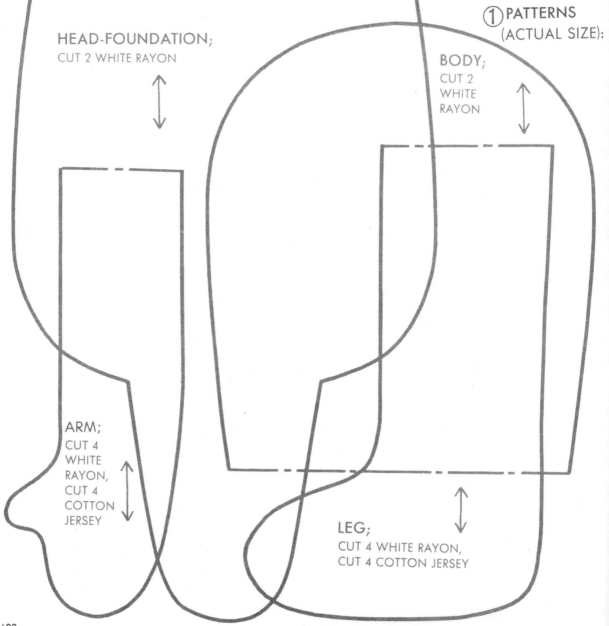

① PATTERNS (ACTUAL SIZE):

HEAD-FOUNDATION;
CUT 2 WHITE RAYON

BODY;
CUT 2
WHITE
RAYON

ARM;
CUT 4
WHITE
RAYON,
CUT 4
COTTON
JERSEY

LEG;
CUT 4 WHITE RAYON,
CUT 4 COTTON JERSEY

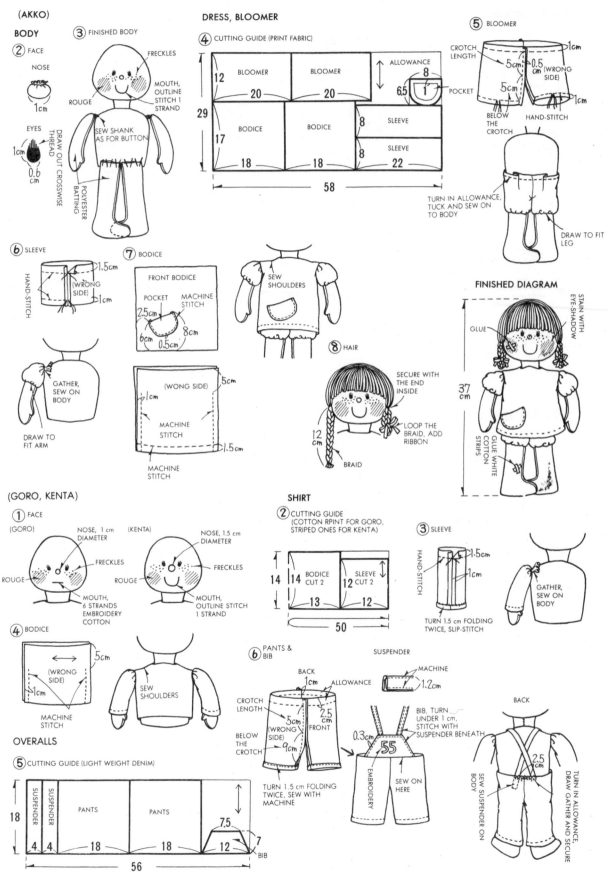

(AKKO)

BODY

② FACE

NOSE

1cm

EYES

1cm
0.6 cm

DRAW OUT CROSSWISE THREAD

③ FINISHED BODY

FRECKLES

ROUGE

MOUTH, OUTLINE STITCH 1 STRAND

SEW SHANK AS FOR BUTTON

POLYESTER BATTING

DRESS, BLOOMER

④ CUTTING GUIDE (PRINT FABRIC)

BLOOMER 12 20
BLOOMER 20
ALLOWANCE 8 6.5
POCKET
29
BODICE 17 18
BODICE 18
SLEEVE 8 22
SLEEVE 8
58

⑤ BLOOMER

CROTCH LENGTH
5cm 0.5cm (WRONG SIDE) 1cm
5cm 1cm
BELOW THE CROTCH
HAND-STITCH

TURN IN ALLOWANCE, TUCK AND SEW ON TO BODY

DRAW TO FIT LEG

⑥ SLEEVE

HAND-STITCH
1.5cm (WRONG SIDE) 1cm

GATHER, SEW ON BODY

DRAW TO FIT ARM

⑦ BODICE

FRONT BODICE
POCKET MACHINE STITCH
2.5cm 8cm
6cm 0.5cm

(WONG SIDE) 5cm
1cm
MACHINE STITCH
1.5cm
MACHINE STITCH

SEW SHOULDERS

FINISHED DIAGRAM

STAIN WITH EYE-SHADOW
GLUE
37 cm
GLUE WHITE COTTON STRIPS

⑧ HAIR

SECURE WITH THE END INSIDE
LOOP THE BRAID, ADD RIBBON
12 cm
BRAID

(GORO, KENTA)

① FACE

(GORO)
NOSE, 1 cm DIAMETER
FRECKLES
ROUGE
MOUTH, 6 STRANDS EMBROIDERY COTTON

(KENTA)
NOSE, 1.5 cm DIAMETER
FRECKLES
ROUGE
MOUTH, OUTLINE STITCH 1 STRAND

④ BODICE

(WRONG SIDE) 5cm
1cm
MACHINE STITCH

SEW SHOULDERS

OVERALLS

⑤ CUTTING GUIDE (LIGHT WEIGHT DENIM)

SUSPENDER SUSPENDER PANTS PANTS
18
4 4 18 18 12
7.5 7
BIB
56

SHIRT

② CUTTING GUIDE (COTTON RPINT FOR GORO, STRIPED ONES FOR KENTA)

14 14 BODICE CUT 2 13
SLEEVE CUT 2 12 12
50

③ SLEEVE

HAND-STITCH
1.5cm 1cm

TURN 1.5 cm FOLDING TWICE, SLIP-STITCH

GATHER, SEW ON BODY

⑥ PANTS & BIB

BACK
1cm ALLOWANCE
CROTCH LENGTH
5cm (WRONG SIDE)
2.5cm FRONT
BELOW THE CROTCH
9cm

TURN 1.5 cm FOLDING TWICE, SEW WITH MACHINE

SUSPENDER

MACHINE
1.2cm

0.3cm
55 EMBROIDERY
SEW ON HERE

BIB, TURN UNDER 1 cm, STITCH WITH SUSPENDER BENEATH

BACK

2.5 cm
SEW SUSPENDER ON BODY
TURN IN ALLOWANCE, DRAW GATHER AND SECURE

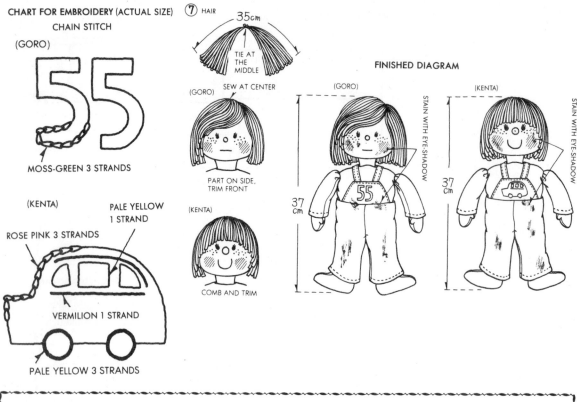

CHART FOR EMBROIDERY (ACTUAL SIZE)
CHAIN STITCH

(GORO)

55

MOSS-GREEN 3 STRANDS

(KENTA)

ROSE PINK 3 STRANDS
PALE YELLOW 1 STRAND
VERMILION 1 STRAND
PALE YELLOW 3 STRANDS

(7) HAIR
35cm
TIE AT THE MIDDLE

(GORO)
SEW AT CENTER
PART ON SIDE, TRIM FRONT

(KENTA)
COMB AND TRIM

FINISHED DIAGRAM

(GORO)
STAIN WITH EYE-SHADOW
55
37 cm

(KENTA)
STAIN WITH EYE-SHADOW
37 cm

MIDORI & OYUKI

Shown on pages 18-19.

Both are made from the same pattern. Create hair styles by combing neatly, and try to use traditional Japanese fabrics.

YOU'LL NEED (for each):
Head-Foundation, Body, Arms, Legs—72 cm by 50 cm white rayon. Face, Nose, Arms, Legs—60 cm by 50 cm cotton jersey. Eyes—dacron georgette. Mouth—strands of embroidery thread. Hair—sport-weight yarn, worsted-weight yarn, 14 cm by 15 cm broadcloth, artificial flowers. Kimono—86 cm by 72 cm cotton fabric. Belt—90 cm by 15 cm broadcloth. Collar—8 cm by 25 cm broadcloth. Also—packing, cotton wadding, polyester batting.
FINISHED SIZE: Refer to diagram.

INSTRUCTIONS:
The basic method is the same as for Hiji, so refer to pages 50-64.
Sew arms on body, setting in properly; then assemble kimono.
Sew collar on body first; make bodice and put on, securing lower half of the front. Make and put on bottom part of kimono. Sew belt, put round the waist hiding all the allowances benath, tie on back.
Sew on hair in same manner as for Hiji, bundle as shown, wrap with fabric piece and secure, putting flowers and decorative band together.

BODY

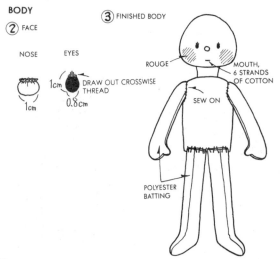

(2) FACE

NOSE   EYES
1cm   DRAW OUT CROSSWISE THREAD
1cm   0.8cm

(3) FINISHED BODY
ROUGE
MOUTH, 6 STRANDS OF COTTON
SEW ON
POLYESTER BATTING

KIMONO

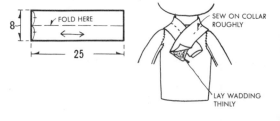

(4) COLLAR (BROADCLOTH)

8
FOLD HERE
25

SEW ON COLLAR ROUGHLY
LAY WADDING THINLY

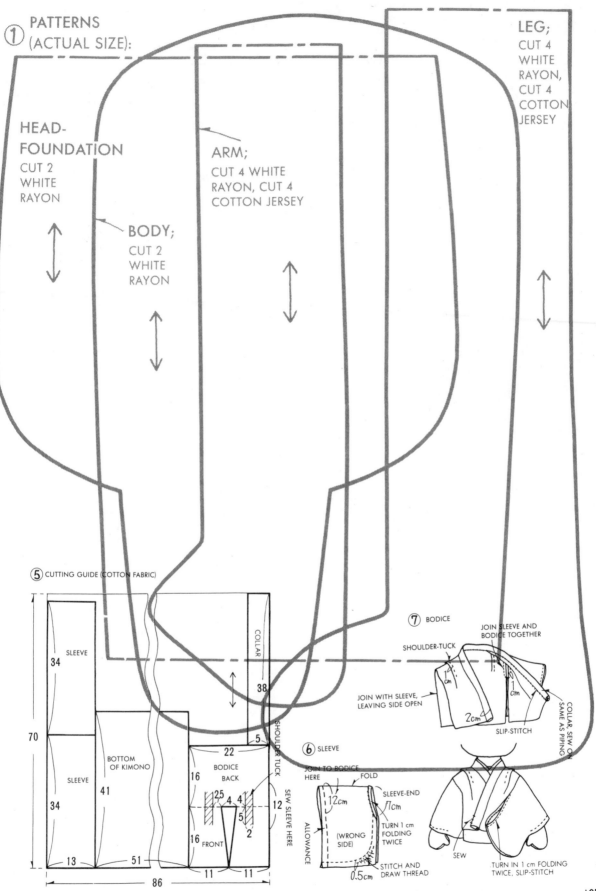

① PATTERNS (ACTUAL SIZE):

LEG;
CUT 4
WHITE
RAYON,
CUT 4
COTTON
JERSEY

HEAD-
FOUNDATION
CUT 2
WHITE
RAYON

ARM;
CUT 4 WHITE
RAYON, CUT 4
COTTON JERSEY

BODY;
CUT 2
WHITE
RAYON

⑤ CUTTING GUIDE (COTTON FABRIC)

SLEEVE
34

SLEEVE
34

BOTTOM
OF KIMONO
41

70

13

51

86

COLLAR
38

5

22

BODICE
BACK
16

25   4   4

5

2

16   FRONT

11   11

SHOULDER TUCK

12

SEW SLEEVE HERE

⑦ BODICE

JOIN SLEEVE AND
BODICE TOGETHER

SHOULDER-TUCK

1cm

1cm

JOIN WITH SLEEVE,
LEAVING SIDE OPEN

2cm

SLIP-STITCH

COLLAR, SEW ON
SAME AS PIPING

⑥ SLEEVE

JOIN TO BODICE
HERE

FOLD

SLEEVE-END
1cm

12cm

TURN 1 cm
FOLDING
TWICE

(WRONG
SIDE)

ALLOWANCE

STITCH AND
DRAW THREAD

0.5cm

SEW

TURN IN 1 cm FOLDING
TWICE, SLIP-STITCH

105

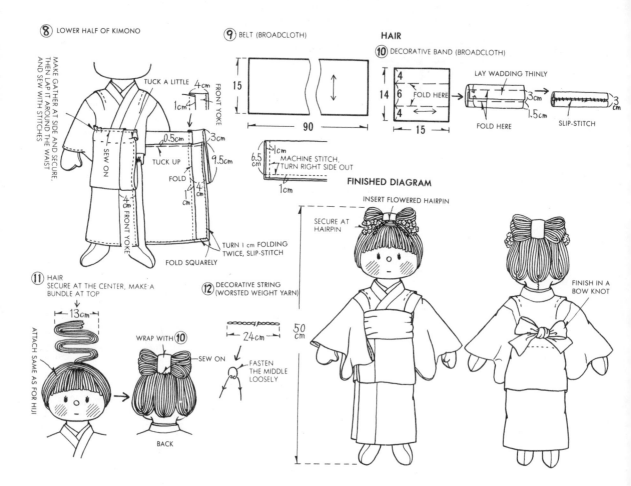

⑧ LOWER HALF OF KIMONO

MAKE GATHER AT SIDE AND SECURE, THEN LAP IT AROUND THE WAIST AND SEW WITH STITCHES

TUCK A LITTLE
4cm
FRONT YOKE
1cm
SEW ON
0.5cm
3cm
TUCK UP
9.5cm
FOLD
4cm
1cm
4cm FRONT YOKE
TURN 1 cm FOLDING TWICE, SLIP-STITCH
FOLD SQUARELY

⑨ BELT (BROADCLOTH)

15
90

HAIR

⑩ DECORATIVE BAND (BROADCLOTH)
4
14 6 FOLD HERE
4
15
FOLD HERE
LAY WADDING THINLY
3cm
1.5cm
SLIP-STITCH
3cm

1cm
6.5cm
MACHINE STITCH, TURN RIGHT SIDE OUT
1cm

FINISHED DIAGRAM

INSERT FLOWERED HAIRPIN
SECURE AT HAIRPIN
50cm

⑪ HAIR
SECURE AT THE CENTER, MAKE A BUNDLE AT TOP

13cm
ATTACH SAME AS FOR HIJI
WRAP WITH ⑩
SEW ON
BACK

⑫ DECORATIVE STRING (WORSTED WEIGHT YARN)
24cm
FASTEN THE MIDDLE LOOSELY

FINISH IN A BOW KNOT

PRINCE & PRINCESS

Shown on pages 20-21.

Put a piece of wire into their arms and legs and pose them as you like. Make a stand of board 2.5 cm or higher, and make a hole with a gimlet to set each foot firmly on the board.

YOU'LL NEED (body materials for both):
Head-Foundation, Body, Arms, Legs—50 cm by 30 cm white rayon. Face, Nose, Arms—33 cm by 28 cm beige georgette. Eyes—dacron georgette. Mouth—strands of embroidery thread. Hair—mohair yarn. Also—wire No. 12, No. 18, packing, cotton wadding, polyester batting.
(Prince): Legs-28 cm by 14 cm silver lamé. Sleeves—24 cm by 16 cm dacron seersucker, 40 cm of 2 cm lace. Bodice, Hat—44 cm by 13 cm purple felt, 100 cm of 2.5 cm braid. Shoes—26 cm of 2 cm black and gold braid, 5 cm by 4.5 cm black felt.
(Princess): Legs, Bloomers—28 cm by 26 cm white georgette, 44 cm of 4 cm lace. Petticoat—40 cm by 11 cm non-woven fabric. Dress—64 cm by 20 cm white lace, 170 cm of 1.8 cm floral braid. 15 cm of 2 cm lace. Hair Ornament, Bouquet—artificial flowers, leaves. 10 cm of 1.8 cm floral braid. Shoes—26 cm of 2 cm pale pink braid. 5 cm by 4.5 cm white felt.

FINISHED SIZE: Refer to diagram.
INSTRUCTIONS:
The basic method is the same as for Hiji, so refer to pages 50-64.
Prince: Make arms and legs with wire inserted in the middle, and connect it with wire inserted into the body.
Make him stand by connecting the wires from the legs to his stand.
Princess: Make body in same manner as for prince, put on underwear and dress.
Sew on hair in the same way as for Hiji, attach back hair of twined yarns. Sew on hair ornament, and let her hold bouquet in the bent hand.

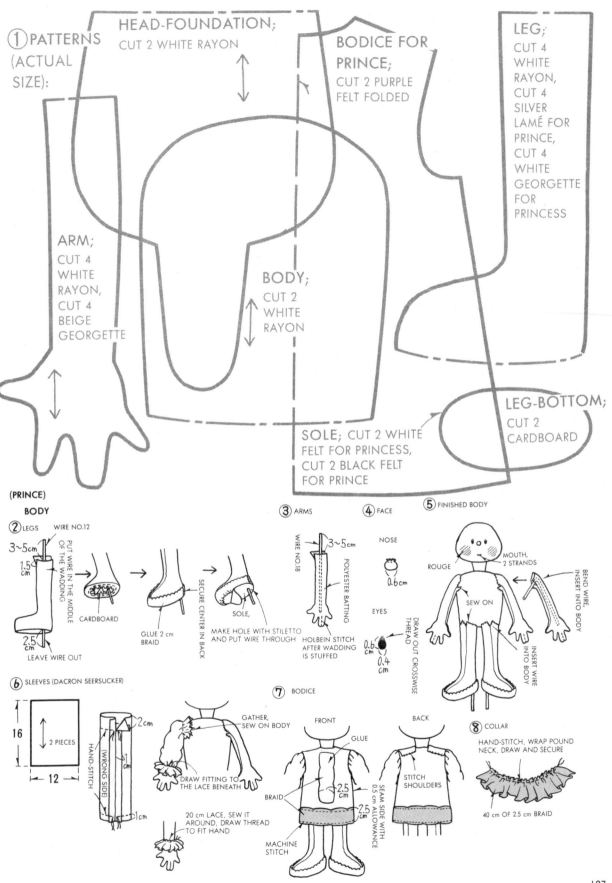

① PATTERNS (ACTUAL SIZE):

HEAD-FOUNDATION; CUT 2 WHITE RAYON

BODICE FOR PRINCE; CUT 2 PURPLE FELT FOLDED

LEG; CUT 4 WHITE RAYON, CUT 4 SILVER LAMÉ FOR PRINCE, CUT 4 WHITE GEORGETTE FOR PRINCESS

ARM; CUT 4 WHITE RAYON, CUT 4 BEIGE GEORGETTE

BODY; CUT 2 WHITE RAYON

LEG-BOTTOM; CUT 2 CARDBOARD

SOLE; CUT 2 WHITE FELT FOR PRINCESS, CUT 2 BLACK FELT FOR PRINCE

(PRINCE) BODY

② LEGS   WIRE NO.12

3~5cm
1.5 cm
PUT WIRE IN THE MIDDLE OF THE WADDING
CARDBOARD
GLUE 2 cm BRAID
SECURE CENTER IN BACK
SOLE,
MAKE HOLE WITH STILETTO AND PUT WIRE THROUGH
2.5 cm LEAVE WIRE OUT

③ ARMS
WIRE NO.18   3~5cm
POLYESTER BATTING
HOLBEIN STITCH AFTER WADDING IS STUFFED

④ FACE
NOSE
0.6cm
ROUGE
EYES
0.6 cm
0.4 cm
DRAW OUT CROSSWISE THREAD
MOUTH, 2 STRANDS

⑤ FINISHED BODY
BEND WIRE, INSERT INTO BODY
SEW ON
INSERT WIRE INTO BODY

⑥ SLEEVES (DACRON SEERSUCKER)
16
12
2 PIECES
HAND-STITCH
(WRONG SIDE)
2cm
1cm
1cm
GATHER, SEW ON BODY
DRAW FITTING TO THE LACE BENEATH
20 cm LACE, SEW IT AROUND, DRAW THREAD TO FIT HAND

⑦ BODICE
FRONT
GLUE
2.5 cm
2.5 cm
BRAID
MACHINE STITCH
BACK
STITCH SHOULDERS
SEAM SIDE WITH 0.5 cm ALLOWANCE

⑧ COLLAR
HAND-STITCH, WRAP POUND NECK, DRAW AND SECURE
40 cm OF 2.5 cm BRAID

107

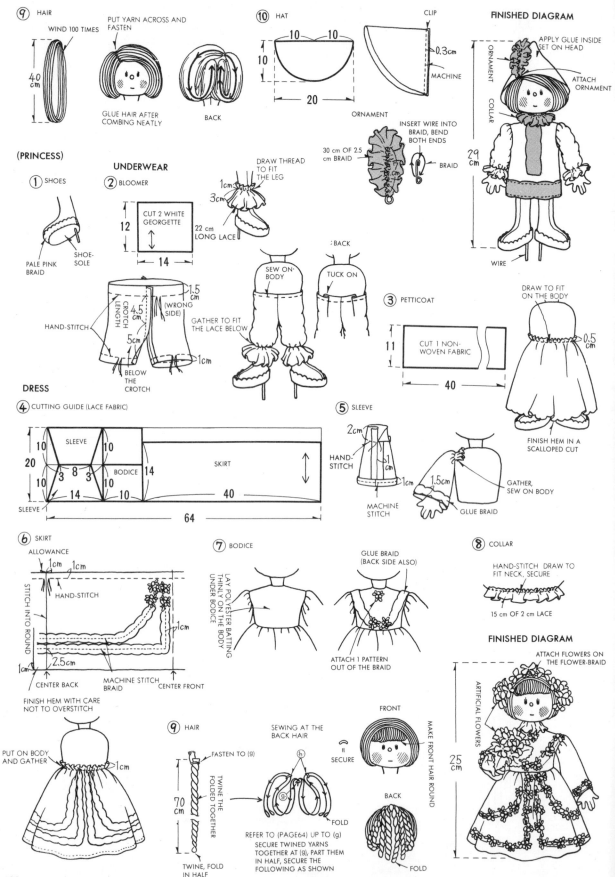

(9) HAIR
WIND 100 TIMES
40 cm
PUT YARN ACROSS AND FASTEN
GLUE HAIR AFTER COMBING NEATLY
BACK

(10) HAT
10 · 10
10
20
CLIP
0.3cm
MACHINE

ORNAMENT
INSERT WIRE INTO BRAID, BEND BOTH ENDS
30 cm OF 2.5 cm BRAID
BRAID

FINISHED DIAGRAM
APPLY GLUE INSIDE SET ON HEAD
ATTACH ORNAMENT
ORNAMENT
COLLAR
29 cm
WIRE

(PRINCESS)

UNDERWEAR

(1) SHOES
PALE PINK BRAID
SHOE-SOLE

(2) BLOOMER
CUT 2 WHITE GEORGETTE
12
14
22 cm LONG LACE
1cm
3cm
DRAW THREAD TO FIT THE LEG

BACK
SEW ON BODY
TUCK ON

1.5 cm
4.5 cm
(WRONG SIDE)
CROTCH LENGTH
5cm
HAND-STITCH
1cm
BELOW THE CROTCH
GATHER TO FIT THE LACE BELOW

(3) PETTICOAT
11
CUT 1 NON-WOVEN FABRIC
40
0.5 cm
DRAW TO FIT ON THE BODY
FINISH HEM IN A SCALLOPED CUT

DRESS

(4) CUTTING GUIDE (LACE FABRIC)
SLEEVE
10 · 10
20
10 · 10
3 · 8 · 3
BODICE
14
14
10
SLEEVE
SKIRT
40
64

(5) SLEEVE
2cm
HAND-STITCH
1 cm
1cm
MACHINE STITCH
1.5cm
GATHER, SEW ON BODY
GLUE BRAID

(6) SKIRT
ALLOWANCE
1cm · 1cm
HAND-STITCH
STITCH INTO ROUND
1cm
2.5cm
MACHINE STITCH BRAID
CENTER BACK
CENTER FRONT
1cm
FINISH HEM WITH CARE NOT TO OVERSTITCH
PUT ON BODY AND GATHER
1cm

(7) BODICE
LAY POLYESTER BATTING THINLY ON THE BODY UNDER BODICE
GLUE BRAID (BACK SIDE ALSO)
ATTACH 1 PATTERN OUT OF THE BRAID

(8) COLLAR
HAND-STITCH DRAW TO FIT NECK, SECURE
15 cm OF 2 cm LACE

FINISHED DIAGRAM
ATTACH FLOWERS ON THE FLOWER-BRAID
ARTIFICIAL FLOWERS
25 cm

(9) HAIR
FASTEN TO (9)
TWINE THE FOLDED TOGETHER
70 cm
TWINE, FOLD IN HALF
SEWING AT THE BACK HAIR
SECURE
FOLD
REFER TO (PAGE64) UP TO (g) SECURE TWINED YARNS TOGETHER AT (9), PART THEM IN HALF, SECURE THE FOLLOWING AS SHOWN
FRONT
MAKE FRONT HAIR ROUND
BACK
FOLD

THE WOOD ELVES

Shown on page 22.

The arms and legs of these very simple dolls move freely. If strings were tied to them, they would become marionettes. Emphasize the humorous expressions in their features.

YOU'LL NEED (for each):
Head-Foundation, Body, Arms, Legs—40 cm by 30 cm white rayon. Face, Arms—70 cm by 22 cm beige cotton jersey. Legs—35 cm by 14 cm striped cotton. Nose—scrap of orange jersey. Eyes—dacron georgette. Mouth—strands of embroidery thread. Hair—heavyweight yarn. Clothes—30 cm by 29 cm olive green felt, 2 of 1.2 cm diameter button. Shoes—16 cm by 8 cm pale yellow felt. Also—packing, cotton wadding, polyester batting.
FINISHED SIZE: Refer to diagram.

INSTRUCTIONS:
The basic method is the same as for Hiji, so refer to pages 50-64.
Make legs with striped fabric, finished in the same way as arms. Color nose fabric with a felttip pen. Sew on hair as shown on page 72, finish front hair in a ladder cut.

① PATTERNS (ACTUAL SIZE):

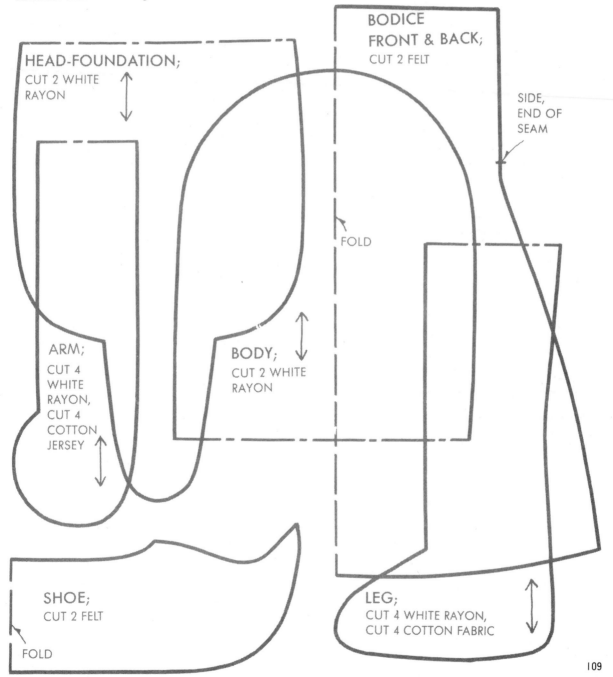

HEAD-FOUNDATION;
CUT 2 WHITE RAYON

BODICE FRONT & BACK;
CUT 2 FELT

SIDE, END OF SEAM

FOLD

ARM;
CUT 4 WHITE RAYON,
CUT 4 COTTON JERSEY

BODY;
CUT 2 WHITE RAYON

SHOE;
CUT 2 FELT

FOLD

LEG;
CUT 4 WHITE RAYON,
CUT 4 COTTON FABRIC

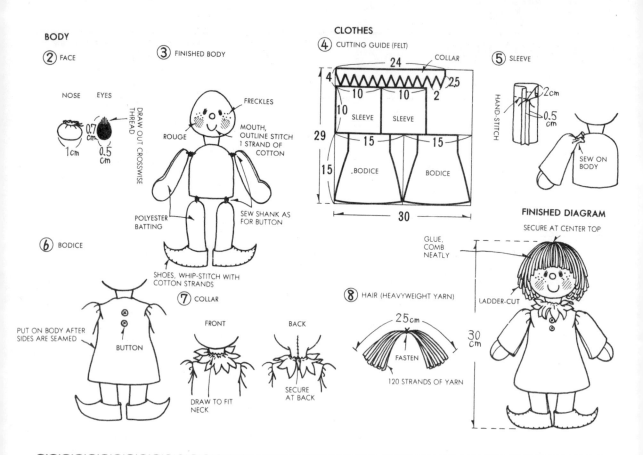

BODY

② FACE

③ FINISHED BODY

NOSE — EYES
1cm / 0.7cm / 0.5cm
DRAW OUT CROSSWISE THREAD

FRECKLES
ROUGE
MOUTH, OUTLINE STITCH 1 STRAND OF COTTON
POLYESTER BATTING
SEW SHANK AS FOR BUTTON

CLOTHES

④ CUTTING GUIDE (FELT)
COLLAR
24
4 / 25
10 / 10 / 2
10 / SLEEVE / SLEEVE
29
15 / 15 / 15
15 / BODICE / BODICE
30

⑤ SLEEVE
HAND-STITCH / 2cm / 0.5cm
SEW ON BODY

⑥ BODICE
PUT ON BODY AFTER SIDES ARE SEAMED
BUTTON

SHOES, WHIP-STITCH WITH COTTON STRANDS

⑦ COLLAR
FRONT
BACK
DRAW TO FIT NECK
SECURE AT BACK

⑧ HAIR (HEAVYWEIGHT YARN)
25cm
FASTEN
120 STRANDS OF YARN

FINISHED DIAGRAM
SECURE AT CENTER TOP
GLUE, COMB NEATLY
LADDER-CUT
30 cm

LOST ANGELS

Shown on page 23.

Arms and legs are finished with wire inside, so pose them as you like. The hair ornament used here is a braid of flowers that you may make.

YOU'LL NEED (for each):
Head-Foundation, Body, Arms, Legs—48 cm by 30 cm white rayon. Face, Nose, Arms, Legs—64 cm by 16 cm cotton jersey. Eyes—dacron georgette. Mouth—strands of embroidery thread. Hair—Lightweight yarn, 20 cm of 1.2 cm floral braid. Clothes—46 cm by 10.5 wool georgette. Wings—13 cm by 6.5 cm white lace fabric, non-woven iron-on interfacing. Also—No. 18 wire, packing, cotton wadding, polyester batting.
FINISHED SIZE: Refer to diagram.

INSTRUCTIONS:
The basic method is the same as for Hiji, so refer to pages 50-64.
Stuff polyester batting into top parts of arms and legs only, insert the wire wrapped with wadding right into the middle. Sew on legs in a sitting position.
Attach the wings of lace fabric pressed with non-woven fabric on back.
Bend hands to make them pose.

BODY

② ARMS, LEGS

③ FACE

④ FINISHED BODY

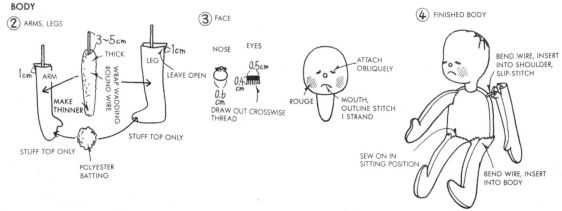

3~5cm / THICK
1cm / ARM / LEG / 1cm / LEAVE OPEN
WRAP WADDING ROUND WIRE
MAKE THINNER
STUFF TOP ONLY
STUFF TOP ONLY
POLYESTER BATTING
STUFF TOP ONLY

NOSE / EYES
0.5cm / 0.4cm / 0.6cm
DRAW OUT CROSSWISE THREAD

ATTACH OBLIQUELY
ROUGE
MOUTH, OUTLINE STITCH 1 STRAND

BEND WIRE, INSERT INTO SHOULDER, SLIP-STITCH
SEW ON IN SITTING POSITION
BEND WIRE, INSERT INTO BODY

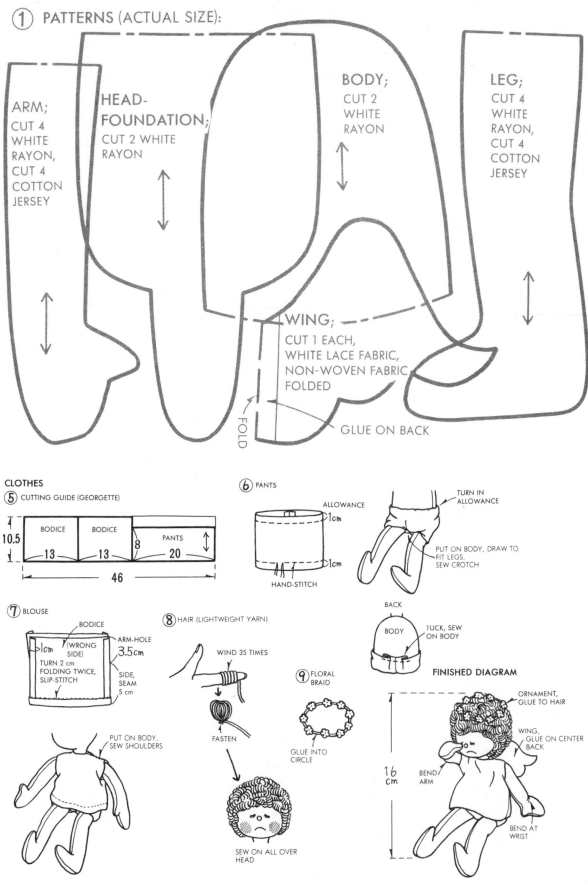

① PATTERNS (ACTUAL SIZE):

ARM;
CUT 4
WHITE
RAYON,
CUT 4
COTTON
JERSEY

HEAD-FOUNDATION;
CUT 2 WHITE
RAYON

BODY;
CUT 2
WHITE
RAYON

LEG;
CUT 4
WHITE
RAYON,
CUT 4
COTTON
JERSEY

WING;
CUT 1 EACH,
WHITE LACE FABRIC,
NON-WOVEN FABRIC
FOLDED

FOLD

GLUE ON BACK

CLOTHES

⑤ CUTTING GUIDE (GEORGETTE)

10.5

BODICE	BODICE		PANTS
13	13	8	20

46

⑥ PANTS

ALLOWANCE
1cm
1cm
HAND-STITCH

TURN IN
ALLOWANCE

PUT ON BODY, DRAW TO
FIT LEGS,
SEW CROTCH

⑦ BLOUSE

BODICE
1cm
(WRONG SIDE)
TURN 2 cm
FOLDING TWICE,
SLIP-STITCH
ARM-HOLE
3.5cm
SIDE,
SEAM
5 cm

PUT ON BODY,
SEW SHOULDERS

⑧ HAIR (LIGHTWEIGHT YARN)

WIND 35 TIMES

FASTEN

SEW ON ALL OVER
HEAD

⑨ FLORAL BRAID

GLUE INTO
CIRCLE

BACK

BODY

TUCK, SEW
ON BODY

FINISHED DIAGRAM

16
cm

ORNAMENT,
GLUE TO HAIR

WING,
GLUE ON CENTER
BACK

BEND
ARM

BEND AT
WRIST

FANTASY

Shown on pages 24-25.

Those are posed dolls, clothed in felt. Make silver flute, wrapping tin foil over a piece of wire. Use same pattern for all fairies. Note the girl's lovely mood.

YOU'LL NEED:

(Each Boy): Head-Foundation, Body—40 cm by 13 cm white rayon. Face, Nose—12 cm by 14 cm cotton jersey. Arms, Legs—48 cm by 12 cm striped cotton. Eyes—dacron georgette. Mouth—strands of embroidery thread. Hair—mohair yarn. Clothes—38 cm by 12.5 cm green felt, 20 cm of 1.3 cm braid. Also—No. 18 wire, packing, cotton wadding, polyester batting.

(Girl): Head-Foundation, Body, Arms, Legs—88 cm by 13 cm white rayon. Face, Nose, Arms, Legs—60 cm by 14 cm cotton jersey. Eyes—dacron georgette. Mouth—strands of embroidery thread. Hair—mohair yarn, 34 cm of 1.8 cm floral braid. Clothes—20 cm by 12.5 cm pale yellow flet, 20 cm of 1.8 cm floral braid. Flute—10 cm of No. 16 wire, Tin foil. Also—No. 18 wire, packing, cotton wadding, polyester batting.

FINISHED SIZE: Refer to diagram.

INSTRUCTIONS:

The basic method is the same as for Hiji, so refer to pages 50-64.

Boys: Make hands and legs with cotton fabric. For the way to stuff hands and legs and the way to set up bodies, refer to page 110. Sew on hair as shown on page 72.

Pose them, bending their arms and legs.

Girl: Make in same manner as for boys. Feature face, secure flute inside her arms.

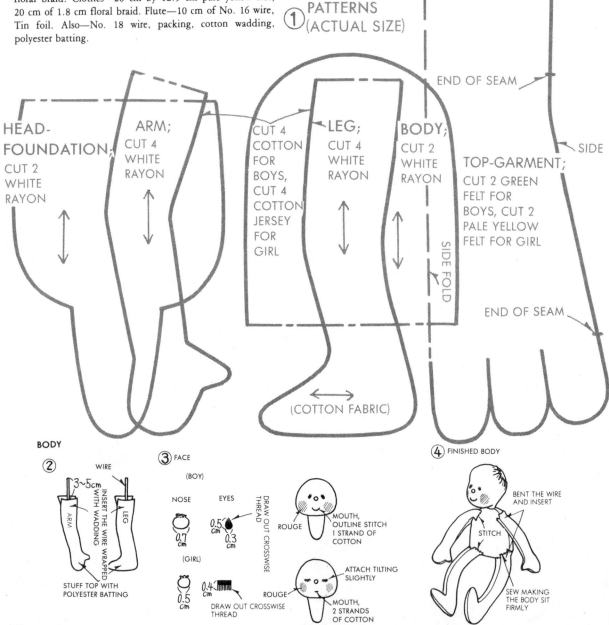

① PATTERNS (ACTUAL SIZE)

HEAD-FOUNDATION; CUT 2 WHITE RAYON

ARM; CUT 4 WHITE RAYON

CUT 4 COTTON FOR BOYS, CUT 4 COTTON JERSEY FOR GIRL

LEG; CUT 4 WHITE RAYON

BODY; CUT 2 WHITE RAYON

SIDE FOLD

END OF SEAM

SIDE

TOP-GARMENT; CUT 2 GREEN FELT FOR BOYS, CUT 2 PALE YELLOW FELT FOR GIRL

END OF SEAM

(COTTON FABRIC)

BODY

② WIRE — 3~5cm — INSERT THE WIRE WRAPPED WITH WADDING — ARM — LEG — STUFF TOP WITH POLYESTER BATTING

③ FACE

(BOY)

NOSE 0.7 cm

EYES 0.5 cm 0.3 cm — DRAW OUT CROSSWISE THREAD

ROUGE — MOUTH, OUTLINE STITCH 1 STRAND OF COTTON

(GIRL)

0.5 cm 0.4 cm — DRAW OUT CROSSWISE THREAD

ROUGE — ATTACH TILTING SLIGHTLY — MOUTH, 2 STRANDS OF COTTON

④ FINISHED BODY

BENT THE WIRE AND INSERT

STITCH

SEW MAKING THE BODY SIT FIRMLY

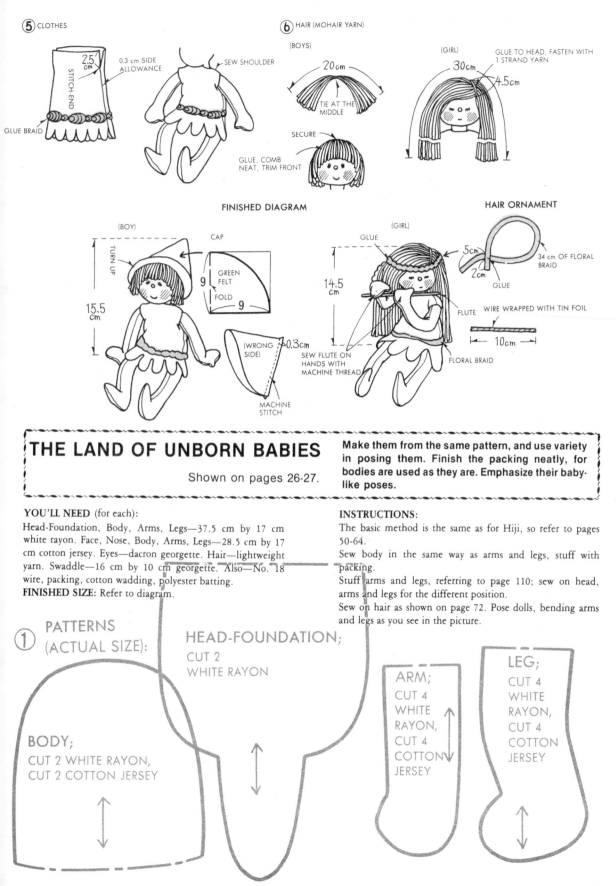

⑤ CLOTHES

2.5 cm
STITCH-END
0.3 cm SIDE ALLOWANCE
GLUE BRAID
SEW SHOULDER

⑥ HAIR (MOHAIR YARN)

(BOYS)
20 cm
TIE AT THE MIDDLE
SECURE
GLUE, COMB NEAT, TRIM FRONT

(GIRL)
30 cm
4.5 cm
GLUE TO HEAD, FASTEN WITH 1 STRAND YARN

FINISHED DIAGRAM

(BOY)
TURN UP
15.5 Cm
CAP
GREEN FELT
FOLD
9
9
(WRONG SIDE)
0.3 cm
MACHINE STITCH

(GIRL)
GLUE
14.5 cm
SEW FLUTE ON HANDS WITH MACHINE THREAD
FLUTE
FLORAL BRAID

HAIR ORNAMENT
5 cm
2 cm
34 cm OF FLORAL BRAID
GLUE
WIRE WRAPPED WITH TIN FOIL
10 cm

THE LAND OF UNBORN BABIES

Shown on pages 26-27.

Make them from the same pattern, and use variety in posing them. Finish the packing neatly, for bodies are used as they are. Emphasize their baby-like poses.

YOU'LL NEED (for each):
Head-Foundation, Body, Arms, Legs—37.5 cm by 17 cm white rayon. Face, Nose, Body, Arms, Legs—28.5 cm by 17 cm cotton jersey. Eyes—dacron georgette. Hair—lightweight yarn. Swaddle—16 cm by 10 cm georgette. Also—No. 18 wire, packing, cotton wadding, polyester batting.
FINISHED SIZE: Refer to diagram.

INSTRUCTIONS:
The basic method is the same as for Hiji, so refer to pages 50-64.
Sew body in the same way as arms and legs, stuff with packing.
Stuff arms and legs, referring to page 110; sew on head, arms and legs for the different position.
Sew on hair as shown on page 72. Pose dolls, bending arms and legs as you see in the picture.

① PATTERNS (ACTUAL SIZE):

HEAD-FOUNDATION;
CUT 2
WHITE RAYON

BODY;
CUT 2 WHITE RAYON,
CUT 2 COTTON JERSEY

ARM;
CUT 4
WHITE RAYON,
CUT 4
COTTON
JERSEY

LEG;
CUT 4
WHITE
RAYON,
CUT 4
COTTON
JERSEY

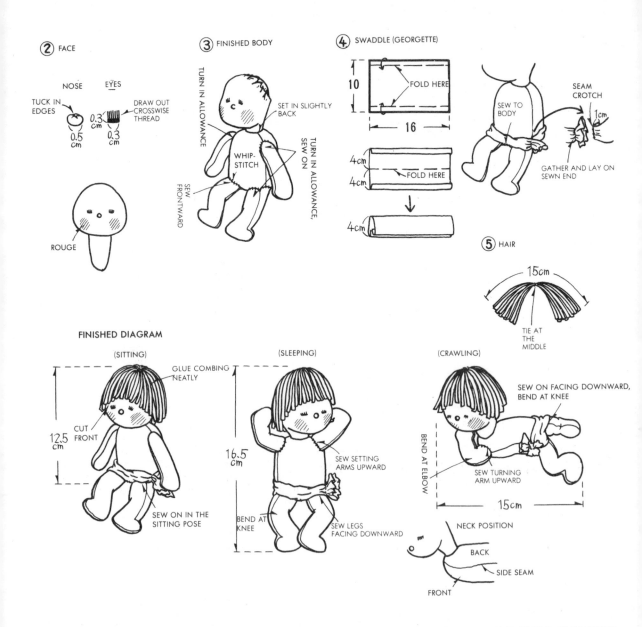

② FACE

NOSE

TUCK IN EDGES

0.5 cm

ROUGE

EYES

DRAW OUT CROSSWISE THREAD

0.3 cm   0.3 cm

③ FINISHED BODY

TURN IN ALLOWANCE

SET IN SLIGHTLY BACK

WHIP-STITCH

SEW FRONTWARD

TURN IN ALLOWANCE, SEW ON

④ SWADDLE (GEORGETTE)

10

16

FOLD HERE

4cm

4cm

FOLD HERE

4cm

SEW TO BODY

SEAM CROTCH

1cm

GATHER AND LAY ON SEWN END

⑤ HAIR

15cm

TIE AT THE MIDDLE

FINISHED DIAGRAM

(SITTING)

GLUE COMBING NEATLY

CUT FRONT

12.5 cm

SEW ON IN THE SITTING POSE

(SLEEPING)

16.5 cm

SEW SETTING ARMS UPWARD

BEND AT KNEE

SEW LEGS FACING DOWNWARD

(CRAWLING)

SEW ON FACING DOWNWARD, BEND AT KNEE

BEND AT ELBOW

SEW TURNING ARM UPWARD

15cm

NECK POSITION

BACK

SIDE SEAM

FRONT

ONDEENA

Shown on page 28.

The choice of materials for hair and dress is the key to making her look nymphlike. Try to get this kind of yarn. Study the balance of arms and legs in the way she is posed.

YOU'LL NEED:
Head-Foundation, Body, Arms, Legs—80 cm by 37 cm white rayon. Face, Nose, Body, Arms, Legs—80 cm by 40 cm cotton jersey. Body—24 cm by 22 cm white georgette. Eyes—dacron georgette. Mouth—strands of embroidery thread. Hair—white lamé yarn, artificial flower. Dress—50 cm by 45 cm white georgette, 17 cm of 1.8 cm braid. Bouquet—artificial flower. Also—100 cm of 0.4 cm ribbon, No. 18 wire, packing, cotton wadding, polyester batting, 13 cm of white elastic.
FINISHED SIZE: Refer to diagram.

INSTRUCTIONS;
The basic method is the same as for Hiji, so refer to pages 50-64.
Make body with white rayon, overlapping cotton jersey and then georgette.
Make arms and legs, referring to page 107. Cut out soles, stitch in place.
Put on dress, belt the waist. Bundle a little of the hair on right side, glue on hair ornament.
Bend arms and legs as shown; sew bouquet on hands, secure legs at knee to steady doll.

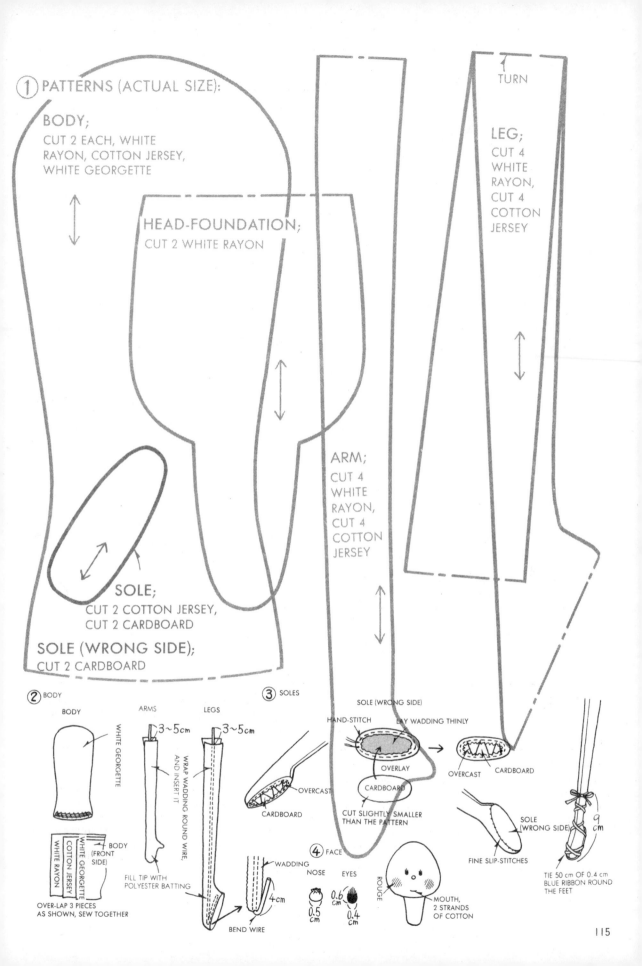

① PATTERNS (ACTUAL SIZE):

BODY;
CUT 2 EACH, WHITE
RAYON, COTTON JERSEY,
WHITE GEORGETTE

HEAD-FOUNDATION;
CUT 2 WHITE RAYON

LEG;
CUT 4
WHITE
RAYON,
CUT 4
COTTON
JERSEY

TURN

ARM;
CUT 4
WHITE
RAYON,
CUT 4
COTTON
JERSEY

SOLE;
CUT 2 COTTON JERSEY,
CUT 2 CARDBOARD

SOLE (WRONG SIDE);
CUT 2 CARDBOARD

② BODY

BODY

BODY

WHITE GEORGETTE

ARMS

3~5cm

WRAP WADDING ROUND WIRE,
AND INSERT IT

FILL TIP WITH
POLYESTER BATTING

LEGS

3~5cm

WADDING

4cm

BEND WIRE

WHITE GEORGETTE
COTTON JERSEY
WHITE RAYON

BODY
(FRONT
SIDE)

OVER-LAP 3 PIECES
AS SHOWN, SEW TOGETHER

③ SOLES

SOLE (WRONG SIDE)

HAND-STITCH

LAY WADDING THINLY

OVERLAY

CARDBOARD

OVERCAST

CARDBOARD

CUT SLIGHTLY SMALLER
THAN THE PATTERN

OVERCAST

CARDBOARD

SOLE
(WRONG SIDE)

FINE SLIP-STITCHES

9
cm

TIE 50 cm OF 0.4 cm
BLUE RIBBON ROUND
THE FEET

④ FACE

NOSE

0.6
cm
0.5
cm

EYES

0.4
cm

ROUGE

MOUTH,
2 STRANDS
OF COTTON

115

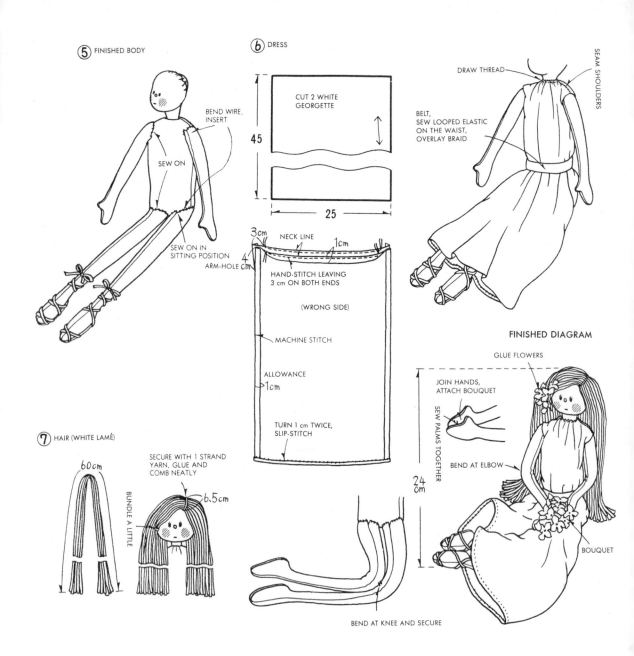

⑤ FINISHED BODY

BEND WIRE, INSERT

SEW ON

SEW ON IN SITTING POSITION
ARM-HOLE

⑥ DRESS

CUT 2 WHITE GEORGETTE

45

25

3cm
NECK LINE
1cm
4 cm

HAND-STITCH LEAVING 3 cm ON BOTH ENDS

(WRONG SIDE)

MACHINE STITCH

ALLOWANCE
1cm

TURN 1 cm TWICE, SLIP-STITCH

DRAW THREAD

SEAM SHOULDERS

BELT, SEW LOOPED ELASTIC ON THE WAIST, OVERLAY BRAID

FINISHED DIAGRAM

GLUE FLOWERS

JOIN HANDS, ATTACH BOUQUET

SEW PALMS TOGETHER

BEND AT ELBOW

24 cm

BOUQUET

BEND AT KNEE AND SECURE

⑦ HAIR (WHITE LAMÉ)

60cm

BUNDLE A LITTLE

SECURE WITH 1 STRAND YARN, GLUE AND COMB NEATLY

6.5cm

PUCK

Shown on page 29.

Stuff packing neatly to give a smooth finish to the body. Emphasize the mischievous spirit of this love-messenger in his features and pose.

YOU'LL NEED:
Head-Foundation, Body, Arms, Legs—60 cm by 32 cm white rayon. Face, Nose—12 cm by 15 cm beige cotton jersey. Body, Arms, Legs—70 cm by 28 cm white cotton jersey. Eyes—dacron georgette, gold lamé yarn. Mouth—strands of embroidery thread. Hair-bouclé. Also—artificial leaves, green taped wire, No. 18 wire, packing, cotton wadding, polyester batting.
FINISHED SIZE: Refer to diagram.

INSTRUCTIONS:
Make body, arms, and legs of white jersey. For the way to make arms and legs, refer to page 107. Attach soles after the green wire is tied round legs. Hair is made of bouclé softly crocheted with single crochet using No. G hook needle, and used on its reverse side. Put polyester batting in the crocheted hair and pull over the head.
Attach leaves to the body, and pose doll by bending arms and legs.

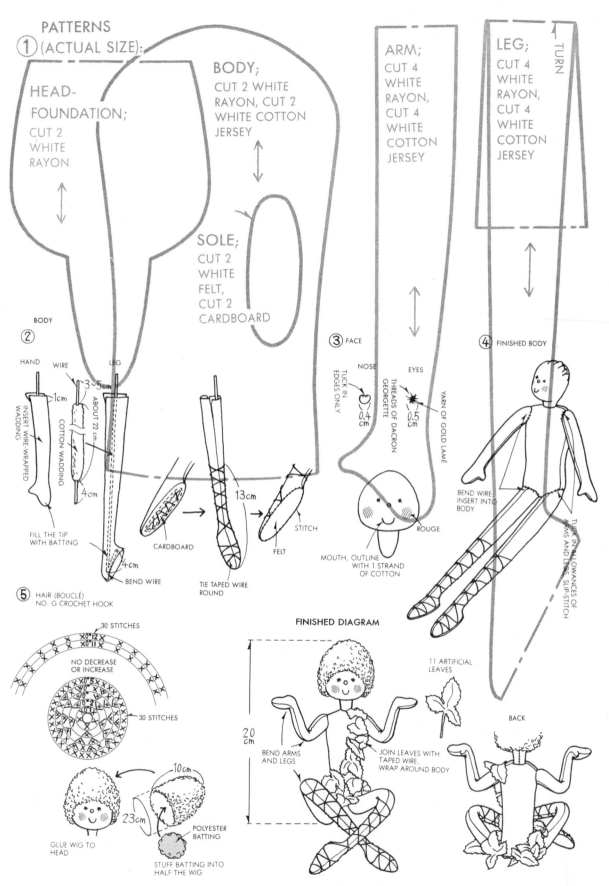

PATTERNS
① (ACTUAL SIZE):

HEAD-FOUNDATION;
CUT 2 WHITE RAYON

BODY;
CUT 2 WHITE RAYON, CUT 2 WHITE COTTON JERSEY

SOLE;
CUT 2 WHITE FELT, CUT 2 CARDBOARD

ARM;
CUT 4 WHITE RAYON, CUT 4 WHITE COTTON JERSEY

LEG;
CUT 4 WHITE RAYON, CUT 4 WHITE COTTON JERSEY

TURN

② BODY

HAND
WIRE
LEG

INSERT WIRE-WRAPPED WADDING

1cm
3~5cm

ABOUT 22 cm

COTTON WADDING

4cm

FILL THE TIP WITH BATTING

CARDBOARD

13cm

BEND WIRE

4cm

TIE TAPED WIRE ROUND

STITCH

FELT

③ FACE

NOSE
TUCK IN EDGES ONLY
0.4 cm

EYES
THREADS OF DACRON GEORGETTE
0.5 cm
YARN OF GOLD LAMÉ

ROUGE

MOUTH, OUTLINE WITH 1 STRAND OF COTTON

④ FINISHED BODY

BEND WIRE; INSERT INTO BODY

TUCK IN ALLOWANCES OF ARMS AND LEGS, SLIP-STITCH

⑤ HAIR (BOUCLÉ) NO. G CROCHET HOOK

30 STITCHES

X0"12X
X0"11

NO DECREASE OR INCREASE

X0"5X
X0"4
X0"3
X0"2
X0"1

30 STITCHES

GLUE WIG TO HEAD

10cm

23cm

POLYESTER BATTING

STUFF BATTING INTO HALF THE WIG

FINISHED DIAGRAM

20 cm

BEND ARMS AND LEGS

11 ARTIFICIAL LEAVES

JOIN LEAVES WITH TAPED WIRE, WRAP AROUND BODY

BACK

PIPPI LONGSTOCKING

Shown on page 30.

Though arms and legs look short in the picture, she really has a smart figure. Insert wire into hair braided on the sides and bend up to give her a rompish look.

YOU'LL NEED:
Head-Foundation, Body, Arms, Legs—90 cm by 30 cm white rayon. Face, Nose, Arms—40 cm by 25 cm beige cotton jersey. Legs—20 cm by 30 cm each, black cotton Jersey, dark brown cotton jersey. Eyes—dacron georgette. Mouth—stands of embroidery thread. Hair—sport-weight yarn. Dress, Bloomer—54.5 cm by 24 cm dotted print cotton, strands of embroidery cotton. Scarf—30 cm by 12 cm cotton print. Also—No. 18 wire, packing, cotton wadding, polyester batting.

FINISHED SIZE: Refer to diagram.
INSTRUCTIONS:
Referring to pages 50-64 for basic method, make legs of black and dark brown respectively.
Tuck garment at center front, sew on decorated pocket, stitch side seams.
Sew on hair in same manner as for Hiji, insert wire into hair braided on sides and bend as shown.
Cut out scarf piece, wrap round neck.
Make shoes sewing on feet, finish by bending their tops upward. Bend legs if you like, securing at the knee back side in same manner as toe.

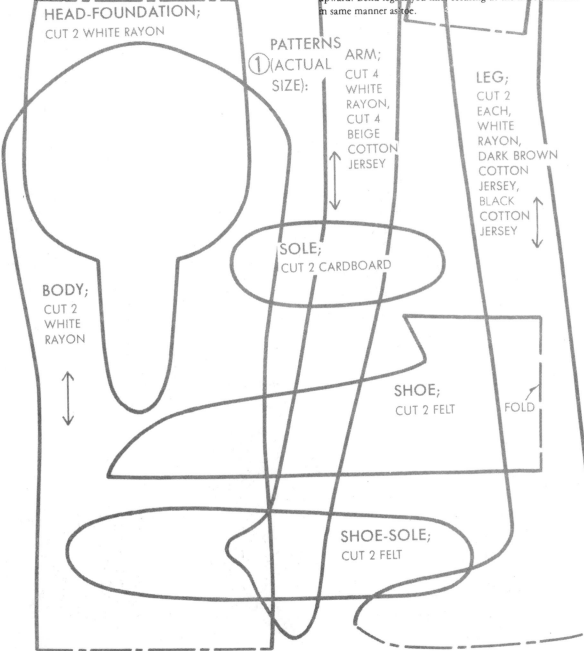

HEAD-FOUNDATION;
CUT 2 WHITE RAYON

PATTERNS
①(ACTUAL SIZE):

ARM;
CUT 4 WHITE RAYON,
CUT 4 BEIGE COTTON JERSEY

LEG;
CUT 2 EACH,
WHITE RAYON,
DARK BROWN COTTON JERSEY,
BLACK COTTON JERSEY

SOLE;
CUT 2 CARDBOARD

BODY;
CUT 2 WHITE RAYON

SHOE;
CUT 2 FELT

FOLD

SHOE-SOLE;
CUT 2 FELT

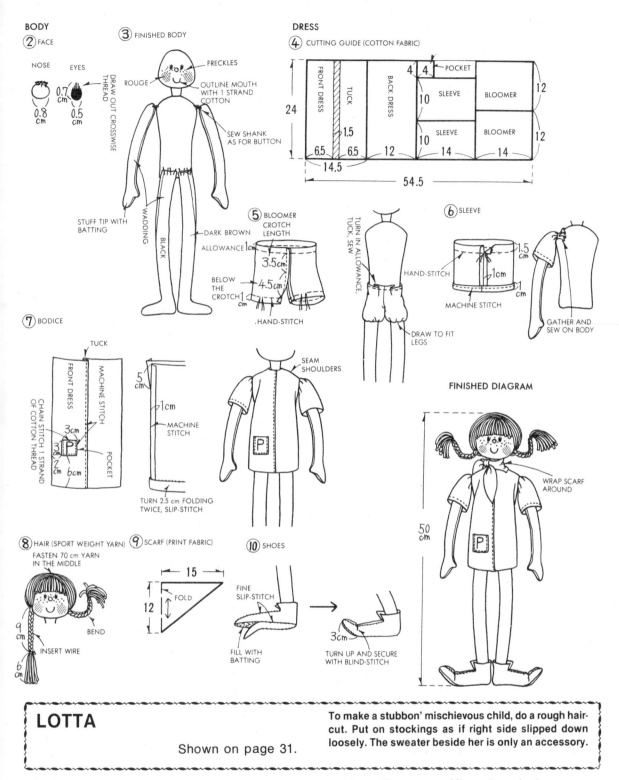

BODY

② FACE

NOSE

EYES

0.7 cm

0.5 cm

0.8 cm

DRAW OUT CROSSWISE THREAD

③ FINISHED BODY

FRECKLES

ROUGE

OUTLINE MOUTH WITH 1 STRAND COTTON

SEW SHANK AS FOR BUTTON

STUFF TIP WITH BATTING

WADDING

DARK BROWN

BLACK

DRESS

④ CUTTING GUIDE (COTTON FABRIC)

FRONT DRESS	TUCK	BACK DRESS	4 4 POCKET		
			SLEEVE	BLOOMER	12
			10		
			SLEEVE	BLOOMER	12
6.5	1.5 6.5	12	10 14	14	

24

14.5

54.5

⑤ BLOOMER

CROTCH LENGTH

ALLOWANCE 1cm

3.5cm

4.5cm

BELOW THE CROTCH 1cm

HAND-STITCH

TURN IN ALLOWANCE. TUCK, SEW

HAND-STITCH

DRAW TO FIT LEGS

⑥ SLEEVE

1.5 cm

HAND-STITCH

1cm

MACHINE STITCH

1 cm

GATHER AND SEW ON BODY

⑦ BODICE

TUCK

FRONT DRESS

MACHINE STITCH

CHAIN STITCH 1 STRAND OF COTTON THREAD

3cm

3 cm

2 cm

6cm

POCKET

5 cm

1cm

MACHINE STITCH

TURN 2.5 cm FOLDING TWICE, SLIP-STITCH

SEAM SHOULDERS

P

FINISHED DIAGRAM

WRAP SCARF AROUND

50 cm

P

⑧ HAIR (SPORT WEIGHT YARN)

FASTEN 70 cm YARN IN THE MIDDLE

9 cm

BEND

INSERT WIRE

6 cm

⑨ SCARF (PRINT FABRIC)

15

12

FOLD

⑩ SHOES

FINE SLIP-STITCH

FILL WITH BATTING

3cm

TURN UP AND SECURE WITH BLIND-STITCH

LOTTA

Shown on page 31.

To make a stubbon' mischievous child, do a rough hair-cut. Put on stockings as if right side slipped down loosely. The sweater beside her is only an accessory.

YOU'LL NEED:
Head-Foundation, Body, Arms, Legs—90 cm by 14.5 cm white rayon. Face, Nose, Body, Arms, Legs—82 cm by 16 cm cotton jersey. Eyes—dacron georgette. Mouth—strands of embroidery thread. Hair—mohair yarn. Shirt, Pants—13.5 cm by 36 cm cotton print. Stockings—lightweight yarn pale yellow, olive green. Sweater—Lightweight yarn gray. Pig—15 cm by 5 cm felt, dacron georgette. Also—No. 18 wire, packing, cotton wadding, polyester batting.
FINISHED SIZE: Refer to diagram.
INSTRUCTIONS;
Referring to pages 50-64 for basic method, make arms and legs in same manner as for Puck on page 117.
Make hair as shown on page 72, finish with laddercut. Additional yarn for hair is attached on sides and back.
Crochet sweater and stockings with size 1 hook.

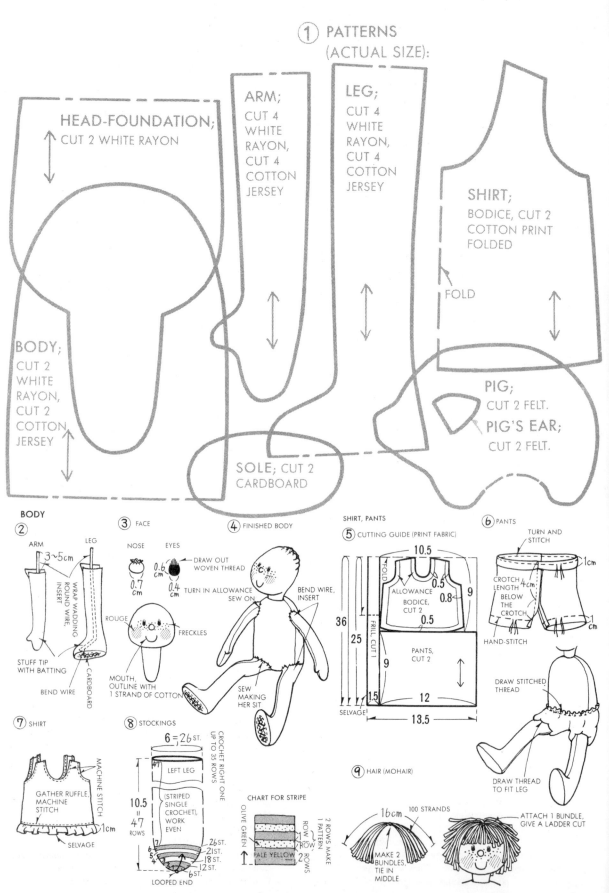

① PATTERNS (ACTUAL SIZE):

HEAD-FOUNDATION; CUT 2 WHITE RAYON

ARM; CUT 4 WHITE RAYON, CUT 4 COTTON JERSEY

LEG; CUT 4 WHITE RAYON, CUT 4 COTTON JERSEY

SHIRT; BODICE, CUT 2 COTTON PRINT FOLDED

FOLD

BODY; CUT 2 WHITE RAYON, CUT 2 COTTON JERSEY

PIG; CUT 2 FELT.

PIG'S EAR; CUT 2 FELT.

SOLE; CUT 2 CARDBOARD

BODY

② ARM LEG
3~5cm
WRAP WADDING ROUND WIRE, INSERT
STUFF TIP WITH BATTING
BEND WIRE
CARDBOARD

③ FACE
NOSE EYES
0.7cm 0.6cm 0.4cm
DRAW OUT WOVEN THREAD
TURN IN ALLOWANCE SEW ON
ROUGE
FRECKLES
MOUTH, OUTLINE WITH 1 STRAND OF COTTON

④ FINISHED BODY
BEND WIRE, INSERT
SEW MAKING HER SIT

SHIRT, PANTS
⑤ CUTTING GUIDE (PRINT FABRIC)
10.5
FOLD
ALLOWANCE
BODICE, CUT 2
0.5 0.8 9 0.5
36 25
FRILL CUT 1
9 12
1.5
13.5
SELVAGE

⑥ PANTS
TURN AND STITCH
1cm
CROTCH LENGTH 4cm BELOW THE CROTCH
HAND-STITCH
DRAW STITCHED THREAD
DRAW THREAD TO FIT LEG

⑦ SHIRT
MACHINE STITCH
GATHER RUFFLE, MACHINE STITCH
SELVAGE
1cm

⑧ STOCKINGS
6=26 ST.
47
LEFT LEG
CROCHET RIGHT ONE UP TO 35 ROWS
(STRIPED SINGLE CROCHET), WORK EVEN
10.5 = 47 ROWS
7 26 ST.
6 21 ST.
5 18 ST.
4 12 ST.
3
6 ST.
LOOPED END

CHART FOR STRIPE
OLIVE GREEN
PALE YELLOW
2 ROWS MAKE 1 PATTERN
ROW 1
ROW 2

⑨ HAIR (MOHAIR)
16cm 100 STRANDS
MAKE 2 BUNDLES, TIE IN MIDDLE
ATTACH 1 BUNDLE, GIVE A LADDER CUT

SWEATER

FINISHED DIAGRAM

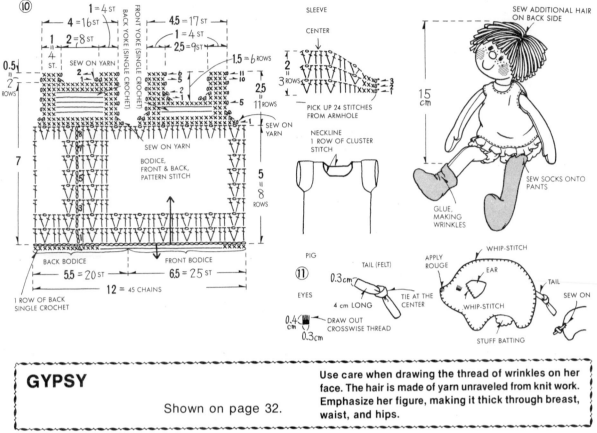

GYPSY

Shown on page 32.

Use care when drawing the thread of wrinkles on her face. The hair is made of yarn unraveled from knit work. Emphasize her figure, making it thick through breast, waist, and hips.

YOU'LL NEED:
Head-Foundation, Body, Arms, Legs—82 cm by 24 cm white rayon. Face, Nose, Arms—35 cm by 17 cm beige cotton jersey. Legs—28 cm by 12 cm black cotton jersey. Eyes—dacron georgette. Mouth—strands of embroidery thread. Hair—white knitting cotton. Bloomer, Petticoat—70 cm by 15 cm white broadcloth, 80 cm of 2 cm white lace. Dress, Scarf—65 cm by 48 cm tricot print. 30 cm of 1.5 cm black lace, heavyweight yarn. Earrings—silver and black braid. Shoes—24 cm of 2.5 cm braid. Stole—No. 30 black lace, Silver lamé yarn. Also—No. 12 silk necklace, No. 18 wire, packing, cotton wadding, polyester batting.

FINISHED SIZE: Refer to diagram.
INSTRUCTIONS:
Referring to pages 50-64 for basic method, make arms and legs in same manner as for Prince on page 107.
Lay wadding over face for more prominent cheeks and jaw; overlay skin fabric and stitch wrinkles with silk thread.
Lay wadding over the breast, waist, and hips to make them thick, sew on underwear and then dress.
Make hair of yarn unraveled from some knit work and attach on the head as shown.
Crochet scarf with a size 8 hook.

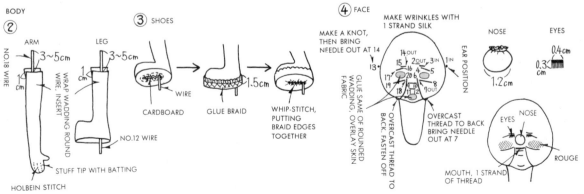

121

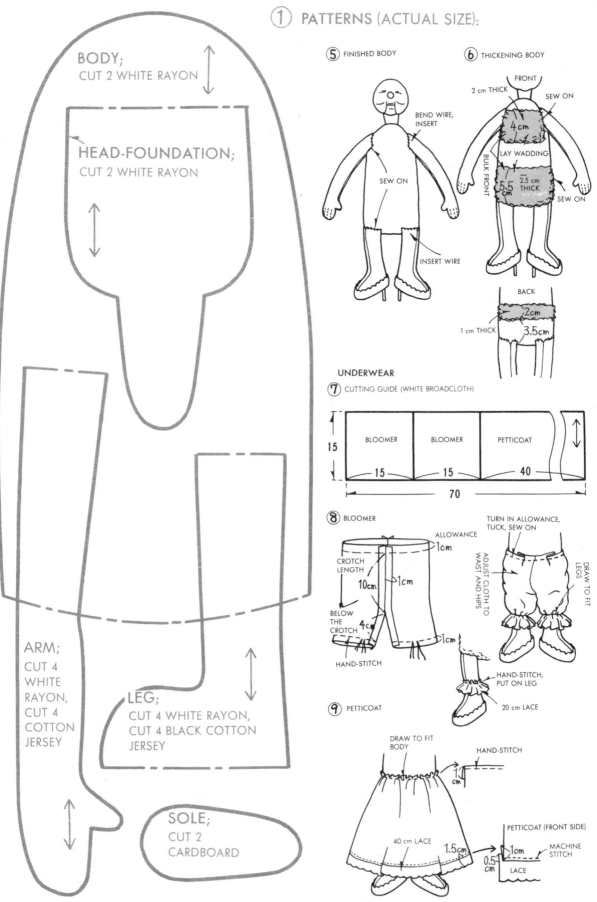

① PATTERNS (ACTUAL SIZE):

BODY;
CUT 2 WHITE RAYON

HEAD-FOUNDATION;
CUT 2 WHITE RAYON

ARM;
CUT 4
WHITE
RAYON,
CUT 4
COTTON
JERSEY

LEG;
CUT 4 WHITE RAYON,
CUT 4 BLACK COTTON
JERSEY

SOLE;
CUT 2
CARDBOARD

⑤ FINISHED BODY

BEND WIRE,
INSERT

SEW ON

INSERT WIRE

⑥ THICKENING BODY

FRONT

2 cm THICK   SEW ON

4 cm

LAY WADDING

BULK FRONT

5.5   2.5 cm
THICK

SEW ON

BACK

2cm

1 cm THICK   3.5cm

UNDERWEAR

⑦ CUTTING GUIDE (WHITE BROADCLOTH)

BLOOMER	BLOOMER	PETTICOAT
15	15	40

15

70

⑧ BLOOMER

ALLOWANCE   1cm

CROTCH
LENGTH

10cm   1cm

BELOW
THE
CROTCH   4cm

HAND-STITCH

TURN IN ALLOWANCE,
TUCK, SEW ON

ADJUST CLOTH TO
WAIST AND HIPS

DRAW TO FIT
LEGS

1cm

HAND-STITCH,
PUT ON LEG

20 cm LACE

⑨ PETTICOAT

DRAW TO FIT
BODY

HAND-STITCH

1 cm

40 cm LACE   1.5cm

PETTICOAT (FRONT SIDE)

1cm   MACHINE
STITCH

0.5
cm   LACE

122

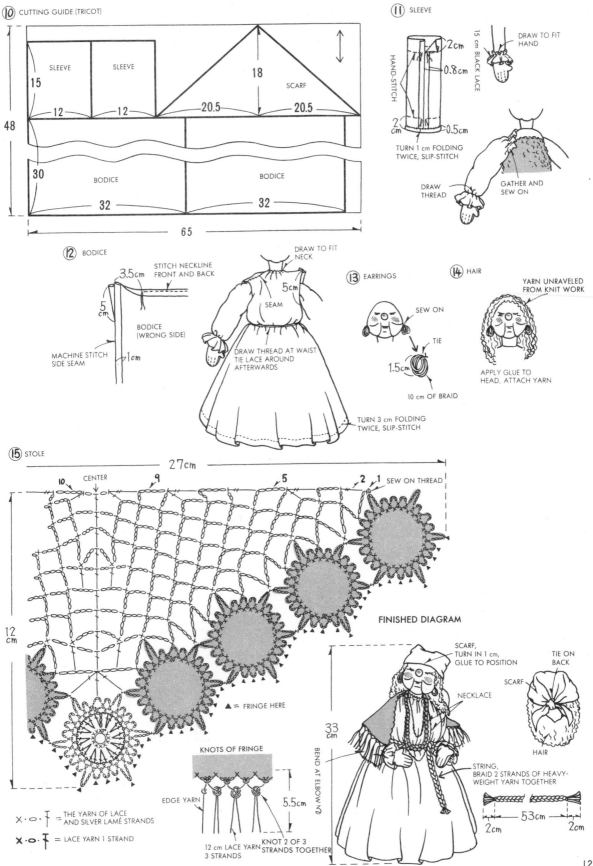

DRESS

⑩ CUTTING GUIDE (TRICOT)

SLEEVE SLEEVE
15
12 12
18
SCARF
20.5 20.5
48
30
BODICE BODICE
32 32
65

⑪ SLEEVE

2cm
0.8cm
HAND-STITCH
15 cm BLACK LACE
DRAW TO FIT HAND
2cm 0.5cm
TURN 1 cm FOLDING TWICE, SLIP-STITCH
DRAW THREAD
GATHER AND SEW ON

⑫ BODICE

3.5cm
STITCH NECKLINE FRONT AND BACK
5 cm
BODICE (WRONG SIDE)
MACHINE STITCH SIDE SEAM
1cm
DRAW TO FIT NECK
5cm
SEAM
DRAW THREAD AT WAIST TIE LACE AROUND AFTERWARDS
TURN 3 cm FOLDING TWICE, SLIP-STITCH

⑬ EARRINGS

SEW ON
TIE
1.5cm
10 cm OF BRAID

⑭ HAIR

YARN UNRAVELED FROM KNIT WORK
APPLY GLUE TO HEAD, ATTACH YARN

⑮ STOLE

27cm
10 CENTER 9 5 2 1 SEW ON THREAD
12 cm
FINISHED DIAGRAM
▲ = FRINGE HERE

KNOTS OF FRINGE

EDGE YARN
5.5cm
12 cm LACE YARN 3 STRANDS
KNOT 2 OF 3 STRANDS TOGETHER

X·○·Ŧ = THE YARN OF LACE AND SILVER LAMÉ STRANDS

X·○·Ŧ = LACE YARN 1 STRAND

SCARF, TURN IN 1 cm, GLUE TO POSITION
NECKLACE
33 cm
BEND AT ELBOW
STRING, BRAID 2 STRANDS OF HEAVY-WEIGHT YARN TOGETHER

TIE ON BACK
SCARF
HAIR

53cm
2cm 2cm

123

THE WITCH OF THE NEW MOON

Shown on page 33.

Her broomstick is made of a tree branch. Try to hang the doll in the air with the string tied on her head, then you can enjoy this flying figure.

YOU'LL NEED:
Head-Foundation, Body, Arms, Legs—77 cm by 25 cm white rayon. Face, Nose, Arms—32 cm by 22 cm beige cotton jersey. Legs—28 cm by 25 cm black cotton jersey. Eyes—dacron georgette. Mouth—strands of embroidery thread. Hair—frizzle yarn. Glasses—black wire. Dress—42 cm by 30 cm black cotton jersey. Cap—19 cm by 16 cm black felt. Broom—45 cm of tree branch, 17 cm square linen. Also—packing, cotton wadding, polyester batting, silk thread, No. 18 wire.

FINISHED SIZE: Refer to diagram.
INSTRUCTIONS:
Referring to pages 50-64 for basic method, make arms and legs in same manner as for Lost Angels shown on page 110. Make wrinkles on her face with silk thread.
Having sewn sleeves on arms, set arms in position. Sew on hair, referring to page 72.

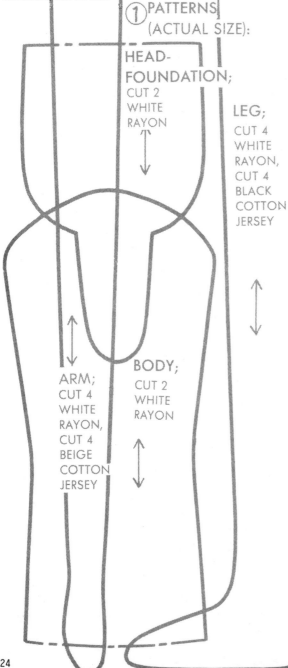

① PATTERNS (ACTUAL SIZE):

HEAD-FOUNDATION; CUT 2 WHITE RAYON

LEG; CUT 4 WHITE RAYON, CUT 4 BLACK COTTON JERSEY

ARM; CUT 4 WHITE RAYON, CUT 4 BEIGE COTTON JERSEY

BODY; CUT 2 WHITE RAYON

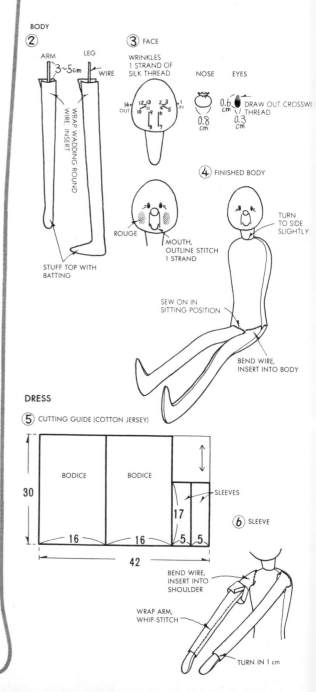

② BODY

ARM   LEG
3~5cm   WIRE

WRAP WADDING ROUND WIRE. INSERT

STUFF TOP WITH BATTING

③ FACE
WRINKLES 1 STRAND OF SILK THREAD

14 OUT   12 13   2 3   1
        10 11 9   7 5   IN
             8 6   4

NOSE
0.8 cm

EYES
0.6 cm   DRAW OUT CROSSWISE THREAD
0.3 cm

ROUGE

MOUTH, OUTLINE STITCH 1 STRAND

④ FINISHED BODY

TURN TO SIDE SLIGHTLY

SEW ON IN SITTING POSITION

BEND WIRE, INSERT INTO BODY

DRESS

⑤ CUTTING GUIDE (COTTON JERSEY)

BODICE   BODICE   SLEEVES

30   17   5   5

16   16

42

⑥ SLEEVE

BEND WIRE, INSERT INTO SHOULDER

WRAP ARM, WHIP-STITCH

TURN IN 1 cm

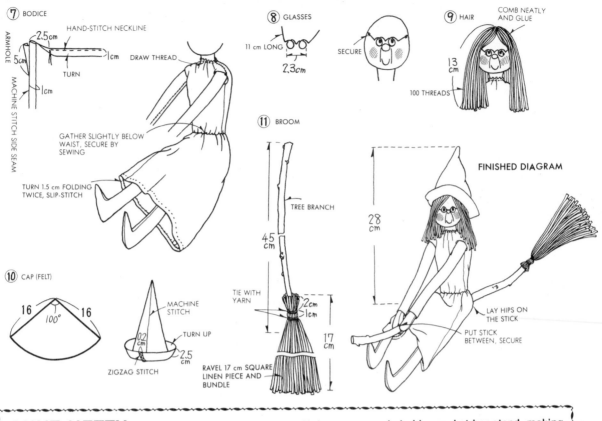

Shown on page 34.

AUNT HETTY

Hairs are unraveled old yarn. Let her stand, making holes on a board 2.5 cm or higher with gimlet. Make wrinkles by drawing thread slightly.

YOU'LL NEED:

Head-Foundation, Body, Arms—47 cm by 27 cm white rayon. Face, Nose, Arms—50 cm by 27 cm cotton jersey. Legs—18 cm by 28 cm striped cotton. Eyes—dacron georgette. Mouth—strands of embroidery thread. Hair—mohair yarn. Glasses—gray wire. Bloomer, Petticoat, Apron, Blouse's collar, Front Placket—59 cm by 23 cm white broadcloth, 51 cm of 2.5 cm white lace, 13 cm of 1.5 cm white lace. Blouse—36 cm by 18 cm cotton seersucker, 25 cm of 3 cm lace. Skirt—30 cm by 25 cm denim. Shoes—26 cm by 3 cm velveteen, 5 cm by 4 cm felt. Also—wire No. 12, No. 18; packing, cotton wadding, polyester batting, silk thread.

FINISHED SIZE: Refer to diagram.

INSTRUCTIONS:

Make according to basic manner on pages 50-64.

Attach skin fabric to face after wadding piece is laid on cheeks and jaw, then stitch wrinkles with silk thread. Make arms and legs with inserted wire. Shoes are made as shown on page 90. For the hair, use the yarn unraveled from knit goods, attaching to the head with glue.

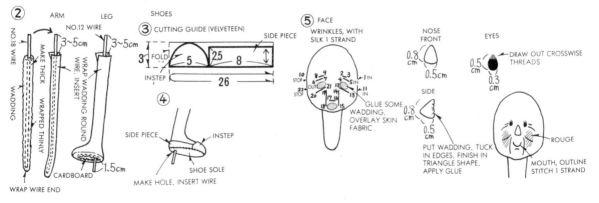

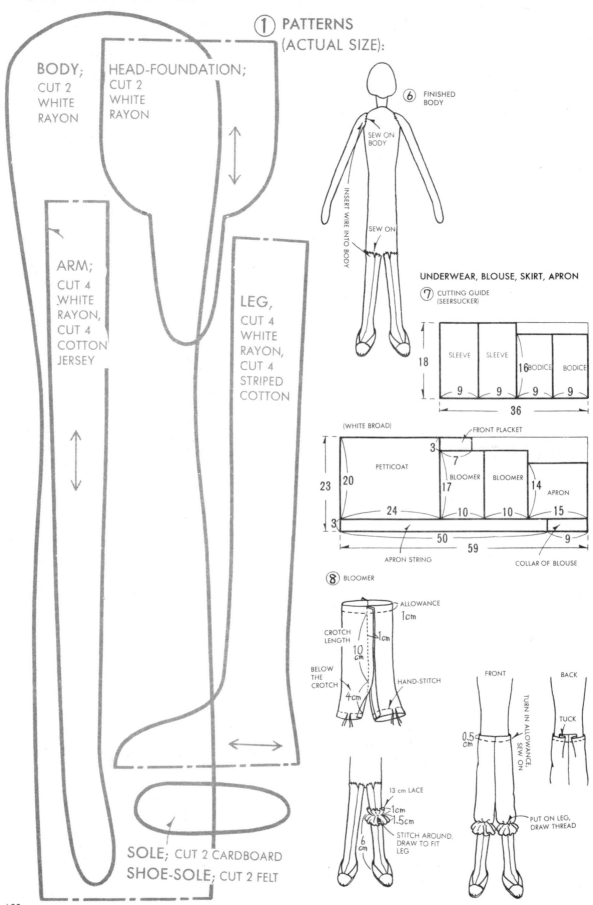

1 PATTERNS (ACTUAL SIZE):

BODY;
CUT 2
WHITE
RAYON

HEAD-FOUNDATION;
CUT 2
WHITE
RAYON

ARM;
CUT 4
WHITE
RAYON,
CUT 4
COTTON
JERSEY

LEG,
CUT 4
WHITE
RAYON,
CUT 4
STRIPED
COTTON

SOLE; CUT 2 CARDBOARD
SHOE-SOLE; CUT 2 FELT

6 FINISHED BODY

SEW ON BODY

INSERT WIRE INTO BODY

SEW ON

UNDERWEAR, BLOUSE, SKIRT, APRON

7 CUTTING GUIDE (SEERSUCKER)

	SLEEVE	SLEEVE	16 BODICE	BODICE
18	9	9	9	9

36

(WHITE BROAD)

FRONT PLACKET

PETTICOAT		3 7		
23 20		BLOOMER 17	BLOOMER	14 APRON
3	24	10	10	15

50

59

9

APRON STRING

COLLAR OF BLOUSE

8 BLOOMER

ALLOWANCE
1cm

CROTCH LENGTH
1cm

10 cm

BELOW THE CROTCH
4cm

HAND-STITCH

FRONT

BACK

TURN IN ALLOWANCE, SEW ON

TUCK

0.5 cm

13 cm LACE

1cm
1.5cm

STITCH AROUND, DRAW TO FIT LEG

6 cm

PUT ON LEG, DRAW THREAD

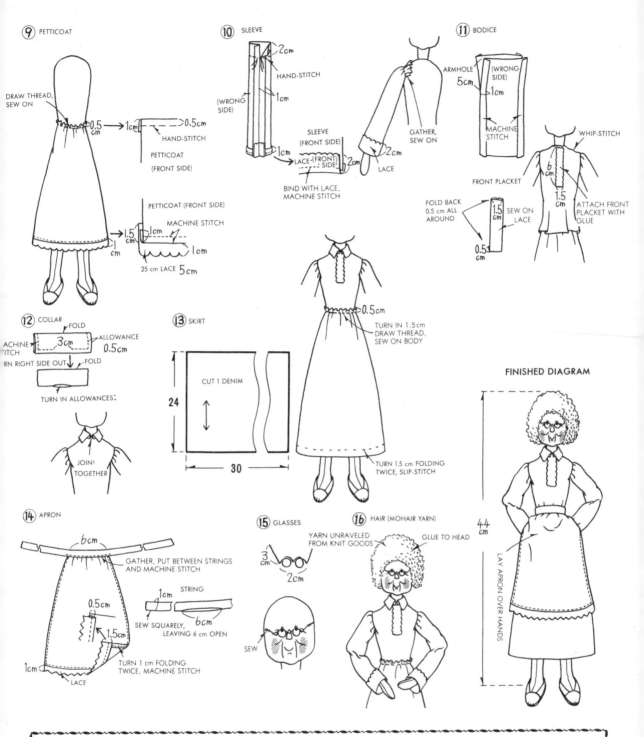

⑨ PETTICOAT

DRAW THREAD, SEW ON

0.5 cm → 1cm → 0.5cm

HAND-STITCH

PETTICOAT (FRONT SIDE)

PETTICOAT (FRONT SIDE)

MACHINE STITCH

1.5 cm — 1cm

1 cm

25 cm LACE — 5cm

⑩ SLEEVE

2cm

HAND-STITCH

(WRONG SIDE)

1cm

SLEEVE (FRONT SIDE)

1cm

LACE (FRONT SIDE) — 2cm

BIND WITH LACE, MACHINE STITCH

GATHER, SEW ON

2cm

LACE

⑪ BODICE

ARMHOLE 5cm

(WRONG SIDE)

1cm

MACHINE STITCH

FRONT PLACKET

WHIP-STITCH

6 cm

1.5 cm

ATTACH FRONT PLACKET WITH GLUE

FOLD BACK 0.5 cm ALL AROUND

1.5 cm

SEW ON LACE

0.5 cm

⑫ COLLAR

FOLD

ACHINE TITCH

3cm

ALLOWANCE 0.5 cm

RN RIGHT SIDE OUT

FOLD

TURN IN ALLOWANCES

JOIN TOGETHER

⑬ SKIRT

CUT 1 DENIM

24

30

0.5 cm

TURN IN 1.5 cm DRAW THREAD, SEW ON BODY

TURN 1.5 cm FOLDING TWICE, SLIP-STITCH

FINISHED DIAGRAM

44 cm

LAY APRON OVER HANDS

⑭ APRON

6cm

GATHER, PUT BETWEEN STRINGS AND MACHINE STITCH

1cm

STRING

0.5cm

6cm

SEW SQUARELY, LEAVING 6 cm OPEN

1.5cm

1cm

LACE

TURN 1 cm FOLDING TWICE, MACHINE STITCH

⑮ GLASSES

3 cm

2cm

SEW

⑯ HAIR (MOHAIR YARN)

YARN UNRAVELED FROM KNIT GOODS

GLUE TO HEAD

MISS BRENDA

Shown on page 35.

The skirt is decorated with white lace attached with shirring. Assembly is basically the same as for Hiji. Make black stockings on her legs by using black georgete as that skin fabric.

YOU'LL NEED:
Head-Foundation, Body, Arms, Legs—86 cm by 58 cm white rayon. Face, Nose, Arms—55 cm by 30 cm beige georgette. Legs—42 cm 35 cm black georgette. Eyes—dacron georgette. Mouth—strands of embroidery thread. Hair—bouclé. Bloomer, Petticoat—82 cm by 29 cm white broadcloth, 50 cm of 2 cm lace. Dress—55 cm by 33.5 cm gingham cheeck, 85 cm by 29 cm gingham smaller check, 630 cm of 2 cm lace ribbon. Shoes—70 cm of 1 cm black braid, 9 cm by 6.5 cm black felt. Also—packing, cotton wadding, polyester batting.

FINISHED SIZE: Refer to diagram.

INSTRUCTIONS:

Make, referring to pages 50-64 for basic method.

Stuff legs firmly with polyester batting.

Sew lace ribbon on the skirt (b), and then shirr it into a piece

55 cm wide.

Stitch shirred lace ribbon to sleeve end, and then sew underarm seam together.

Sew hair all over head in the same manner as shown on page 67.

① PATTERNS (ACTUAL SIZE):

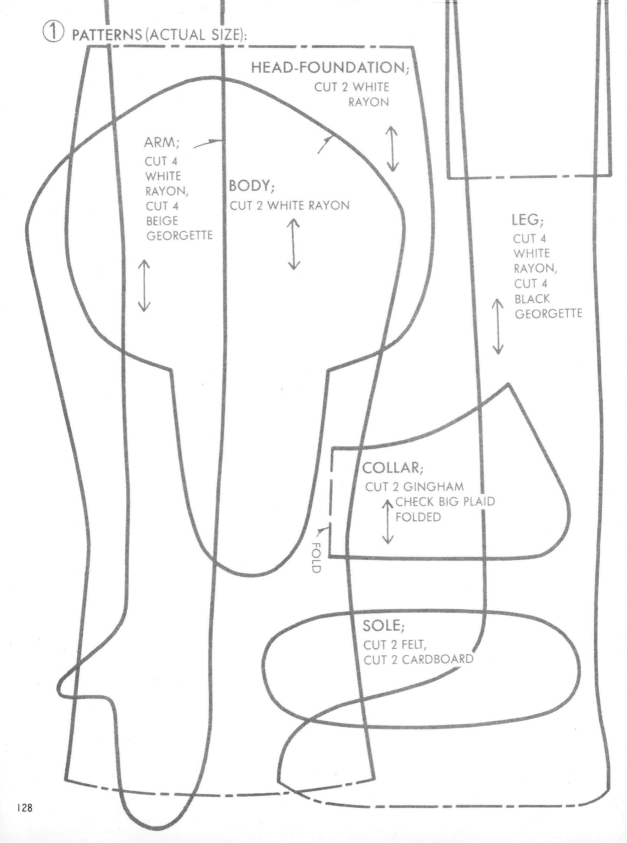

HEAD-FOUNDATION;
CUT 2 WHITE RAYON

ARM;
CUT 4 WHITE RAYON, CUT 4 BEIGE GEORGETTE

BODY;
CUT 2 WHITE RAYON

LEG;
CUT 4 WHITE RAYON, CUT 4 BLACK GEORGETTE

COLLAR;
CUT 2 GINGHAM CHECK BIG PLAID FOLDED

FOLD

SOLE;
CUT 2 FELT, CUT 2 CARDBOARD

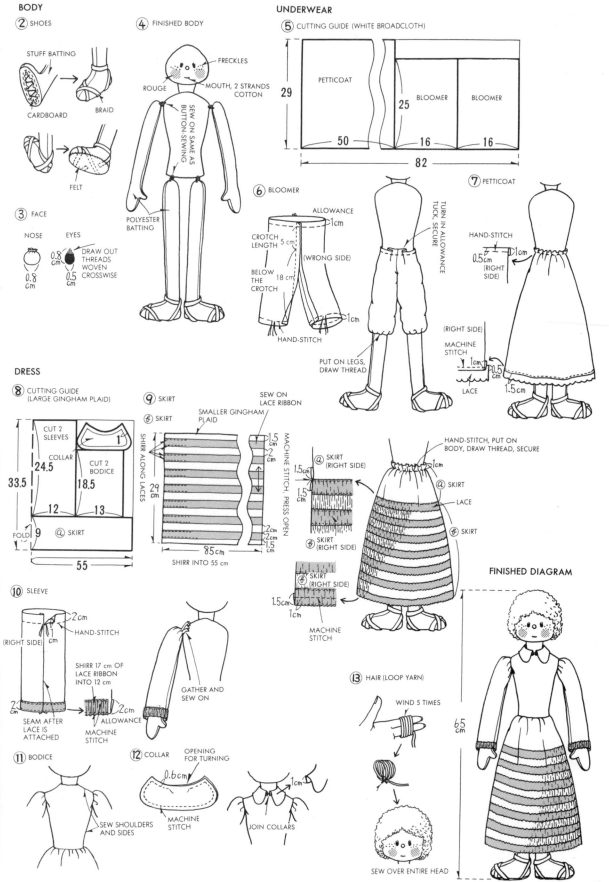

BODY

② SHOES

STUFF BATTING

CARDBOARD

BRAID

FELT

③ FACE

NOSE

0.8 cm

EYES

0.8 cm

0.5 cm

DRAW OUT THREADS WOVEN CROSSWISE

④ FINISHED BODY

FRECKLES

ROUGE

MOUTH, 2 STRANDS COTTON

SEW ON SAME AS BUTTON-SEWING

POLYESTER BATTING

UNDERWEAR

⑤ CUTTING GUIDE (WHITE BROADCLOTH)

PETTICOAT

29

50

25

BLOOMER

16

BLOOMER

16

82

⑥ BLOOMER

ALLOWANCE 1cm

CROTCH LENGTH 5 cm

(WRONG SIDE)

BELOW THE CROTCH 18 cm

1cm

HAND-STITCH

TURN IN ALLOWANCE TUCK, SECURE

PUT ON LEGS, DRAW THREAD

⑦ PETTICOAT

HAND-STITCH

0.5cm 1cm (RIGHT SIDE)

(RIGHT SIDE)

MACHINE STITCH

1cm 0.5

LACE 1.5cm

DRESS

⑧ CUTTING GUIDE (LARGE GINGHAM PLAID)

CUT 2 SLEEVES

COLLAR

24.5

18.5

CUT 2 BODICE

33.5

12

13

FOLD 9

ⓐ SKIRT

55

⑨ SKIRT

ⓑ SKIRT

SMALLER GINGHAM PLAID

SHIRR ALONG LACES

29 cm

SEW ON LACE RIBBON

1.5 cm

2 cm

2cm

2cm

1.5 cm

MACHINE STITCH, PRESS OPEN

85cm

SHIRR INTO 55 cm

ⓐ SKIRT (RIGHT SIDE)

1.5cm

1.5cm

ⓑ SKIRT (RIGHT SIDE)

ⓑ SKIRT (RIGHT SIDE)

1.5cm

1cm

MACHINE STITCH

HAND-STITCH, PUT ON BODY, DRAW THREAD, SECURE

1cm

ⓐ SKIRT

LACE

ⓑ SKIRT

⑩ SLEEVE

2cm

HAND-STITCH

(RIGHT SIDE)

2 cm

SEAM AFTER LACE IS ATTACHED

2cm

ALLOWANCE

MACHINE STITCH

SHIRR 17 cm OF LACE RIBBON INTO 12 cm

GATHER AND SEW ON

⑪ BODICE

SEW SHOULDERS AND SIDES

⑫ COLLAR

OPENING FOR TURNING

0.6cm

MACHINE STITCH

1cm

JOIN COLLARS

⑬ HAIR (LOOP YARN)

WIND 5 TIMES

SEW OVER ENTIRE HEAD

FINISHED DIAGRAM

65 cm

129

AT HOME ON A RAINY DAY

Shown on page 37.

The way of her legs is special for this doll. Use a fine thread of skin color. Fix her position when making the foundation. Set in head with the face turned slightly sideways.

YOU'LL NEED:
Head-Foundation, Body, Arms, Legs—80 cm by 38 cm white rayon. Face, Nose, Arms, Legs—70 cm by 30 cm cotton jersey. Eyes—dacron georgette. Mouth—strands of embroidery thread. Hair—sport-weight yarn. Kimono—77 cm by 30 cm cotton print. Belt—72 cm by 10 cm broadcloth. Also—No. 18 wire, packing, cotton wadding, polyester batting.

FINISHED SIZE: Refer to diagram.

INSTRUCTIONS:
Referring to pages 50-64 for basic method, make arms and legs in same manner as for Puck, shown on page 117.
Make but with the big toes sewn on top as shown.
Sew kimono, referring to pages 105-106, tie belt round, position her by bending arms and legs.
Sew on hair as shown on page 72.

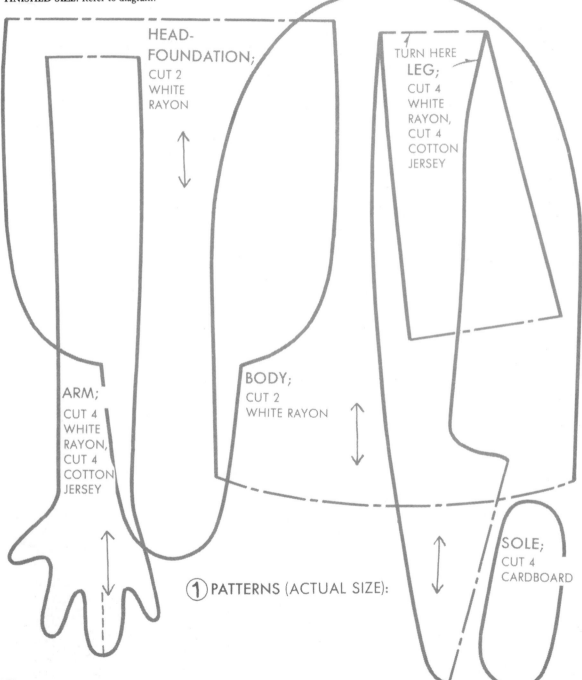

HEAD-
FOUNDATION;
CUT 2
WHITE
RAYON

TURN HERE
LEG;
CUT 4
WHITE
RAYON,
CUT 4
COTTON
JERSEY

ARM;
CUT 4
WHITE
RAYON,
CUT 4
COTTON
JERSEY

BODY;
CUT 2
WHITE RAYON

SOLE;
CUT 4
CARDBOARD

① PATTERNS (ACTUAL SIZE):

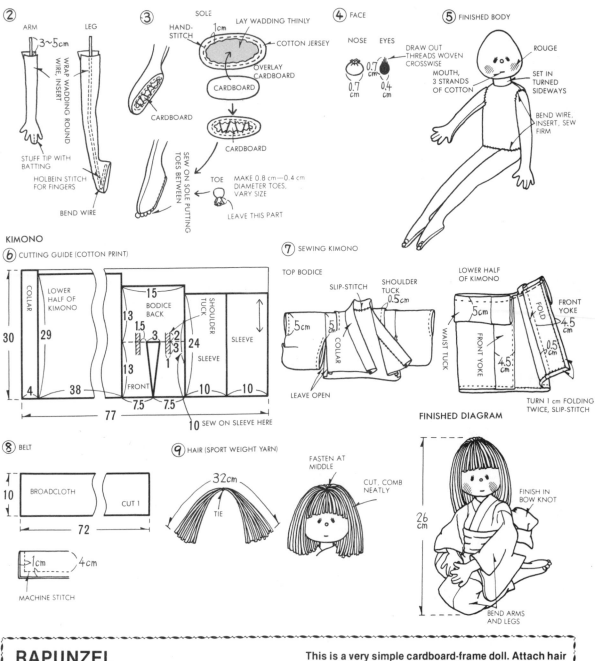

RAPUNZEL

Shown on page 38.

This is a very simple cardboard-frame doll. Attach hair of embroidery floss or a bright yellow yarn, combing neatly with a tooth brush or similar tool.

YOU'LL NEED:
Head-Foundation, Body, Arms—60 cm by 13 cm white rayon. Face, Nose, Arms—40 cm by 14 cm cotton jersey. Frame—26 cm by 18 cm cardboard, 35 cm by 20 cm white rayon. Eyes—dacron georgette. Mouth—strands of embroidery thread. Hair—strands of embroidery cotton 3 shades of yellow, floral braid. Petticoat—40 cm by 14 cm white broadcloth, 40 cm of 2 cm lace. Dress—44 cm by 44 cm cotton print, strands of embroidery thread. Apron—12 cm by 11 cm dacron seersucker, 95 cm of 2 cm lace. Also— No. 18 wire, packing, cotton wadding, polyester batting.
FINISHED SIZE: Refer to diagram.

INSTRUCTIONS:
Make according to basic method on pages 50-64. For the way to form and to set in arms, refer to page 110.

Make frame and sew on body. Sew frame cover, lay on the frame as shown.

Lay wadding thinly over the body, sew on bodice and work cross-stitch at center front.

Sew apron on waist, put lace ribbon over it, glue and tie at back.

Make hair by putting 3 shades of embroidery cotton together, fasten in the middle, secure to head. Make hair ornament and attach to the hair.

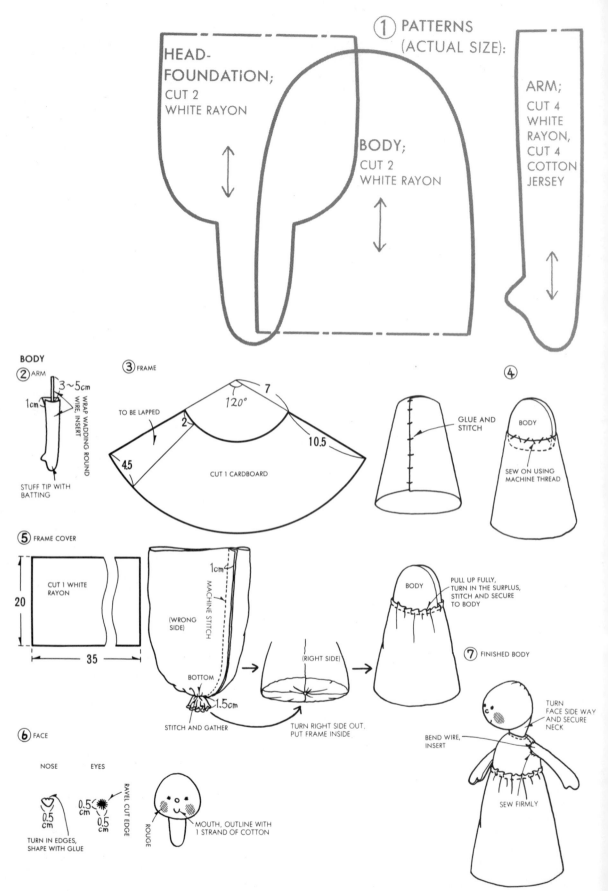

① PATTERNS (ACTUAL SIZE):

HEAD-FOUNDATION; CUT 2 WHITE RAYON

BODY; CUT 2 WHITE RAYON

ARM; CUT 4 WHITE RAYON, CUT 4 COTTON JERSEY

BODY

② ARM
3~5cm
1cm
WRAP WADDING ROUND WIRE, INSERT
STUFF TIP WITH BATTING

③ FRAME
120°
7
TO BE LAPPED
2
4.5
10.5
CUT 1 CARDBOARD

④
GLUE AND STITCH
BODY
SEW ON USING MACHINE THREAD

⑤ FRAME COVER
CUT 1 WHITE RAYON
20
35
1cm
MACHINE STITCH
(WRONG SIDE)
BOTTOM
STITCH AND GATHER
1.5cm
(RIGHT SIDE)
TURN RIGHT SIDE OUT, PUT FRAME INSIDE
BODY
PULL UP FULLY, TURN IN THE SURPLUS, STITCH AND SECURE TO BODY

⑦ FINISHED BODY
TURN FACE SIDE WAY AND SECURE NECK
BEND WIRE, INSERT
SEW FIRMLY

⑥ FACE
NOSE
0.5 cm
TURN IN EDGES, SHAPE WITH GLUE
EYES
0.5 cm
0.5 cm
RAVEL CUT EDGE
ROUGE
MOUTH, OUTLINE WITH 1 STRAND OF COTTON

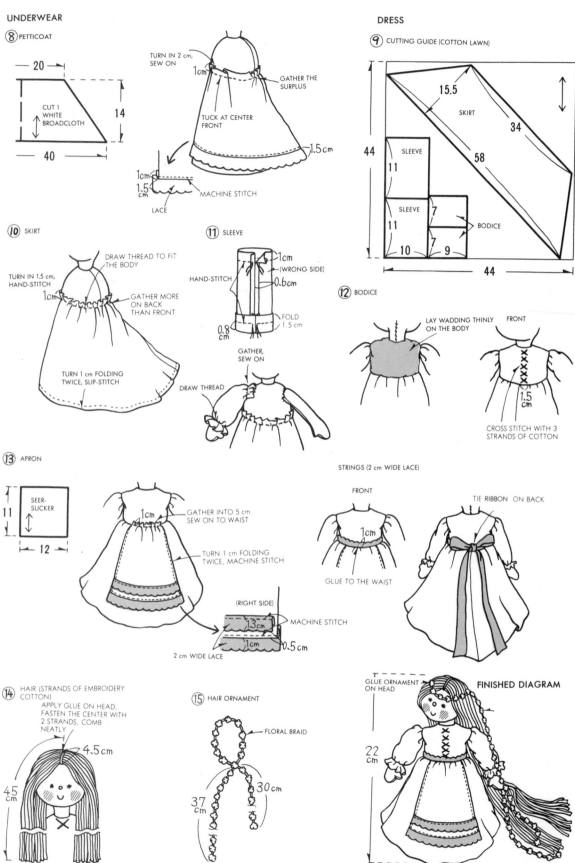

UNDERWEAR

⑧ PETTICOAT

— 20 —

CUT 1 WHITE BROADCLOTH

14

— 40 —

TURN IN 2 cm, SEW ON

1cm

GATHER THE SURPLUS

TUCK AT CENTER FRONT

1.5 cm

1cm
1.5 cm

MACHINE STITCH

LACE

⑩ SKIRT

TURN IN 1.5 cm, HAND-STITCH

1cm

DRAW THREAD TO FIT THE BODY

GATHER MORE ON BACK THAN FRONT

TURN 1 cm FOLDING TWICE, SLIP-STITCH

⑪ SLEEVE

HAND-STITCH

1cm
(WRONG SIDE)
0.6cm

FOLD
1.5 cm

0.8 cm

GATHER, SEW ON

DRAW THREAD

⑬ APRON

SEER-SUCKER

11

— 12 —

1cm

GATHER INTO 5 cm SEW ON TO WAIST

TURN 1 cm FOLDING TWICE, MACHINE STITCH

(RIGHT SIDE)

1.3 cm
1cm
0.5 cm

MACHINE STITCH

2 cm WIDE LACE

⑭ HAIR (STRANDS OF EMBROIDERY COTTON)

APPLY GLUE ON HEAD, FASTEN THE CENTER WITH 2 STRANDS, COMB NEATLY

4.5 cm

45 cm

⑮ HAIR ORNAMENT

FLORAL BRAID

30 cm

37 cm

DRESS

⑨ CUTTING GUIDE (COTTON LAWN)

15.5

SKIRT

34

58

44

SLEEVE
11

SLEEVE
11

10

7

7

9

BODICE

44

⑫ BODICE

LAY WADDING THINLY ON THE BODY

FRONT

1.5 cm

CROSS STITCH WITH 3 STRANDS OF COTTON

STRINGS (2 cm WIDE LACE)

FRONT

1cm

GLUE TO THE WAIST

TIE RIBBON ON BACK

GLUE ORNAMENT ON HEAD

FINISHED DIAGRAM

22 cm

133

PRINCESS ELISSA

Shown on page 39.

Use thick cardboard for the frame if it is availabe. Make the doll most princesslike, using gorgeous fabrics and fancy ribbons.

YOU'LL NEED:

Head-Foundation, Body, Arms—45 cm by 23 cm white rayon. Face, Nose, Arms—30 cm by 22 cm georgette. Frame—33 cm by 33 cm cardboard, 40 cm by 35 cm white rayon. Eyes—dacron georgette. Mouth—strands of embroidery thread. Hair—strands embroidery thread, 210 cm of 3.5 cm lace ribbon, artificial flower. Petticoat—55 cm by 29 cm non-woven fabric. Dress—90 cm by 51 cm lace fabric, 90 cm by 44cm pink lining, 130 cm of 3.5 cm lace ribbon, artificial flower. Also—No. 18 wire, packing, cotton wadding, polyester batting.

FINISHED SIZE: Refer to diagram.

INSTRUCTIONS:

Referring to pages 50-64 for basic method, make arms in same manner as for Lost Angels on page 110; make frame as shown on page 132.

Lay wadding on the body in same manner as for Rapunzel on page 132; sew on bodice with the lining beneath. Sew skirt and then its lining securing 2 pieces together at waist. Decorate front of neck and apply flowers on the skirt.

Position her with the arm bent, glue sleeve ends together.

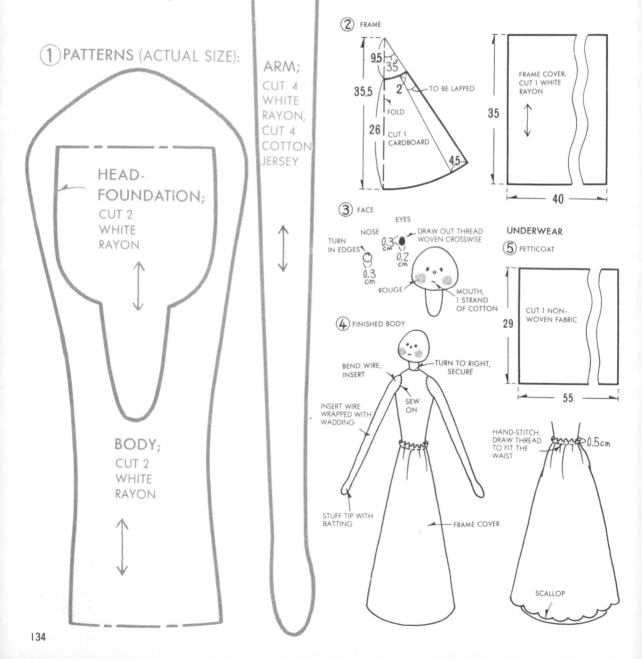

DRESS

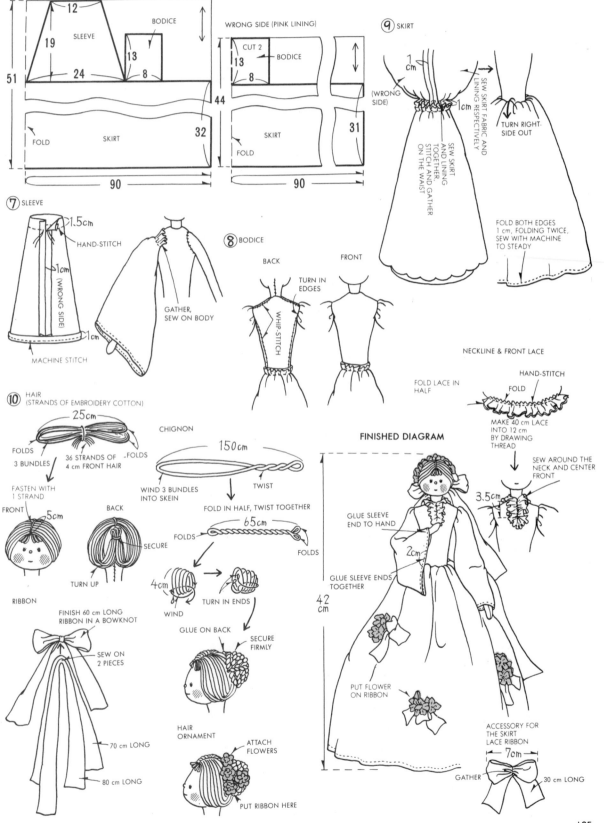

⑥ CUTTING GUIDE
RIGHT SIDE (LACE FABRIC)

12
19
SLEEVE
BODICE
13
51
24
8
FOLD
SKIRT
44
32
90

WRONG SIDE (PINK LINING)
CUT 2
13
BODICE
8
(WRONG SIDE)
SKIRT
FOLD
31
90

⑨ SKIRT
1 cm
(WRONG SIDE)
1 cm
SEW SKIRT FABRIC AND LINING RESPECTIVELY
SEW SKIRT AND LINING TOGETHER, STITCH AND GATHER ON THE WAIST
TURN RIGHT-SIDE OUT
FOLD BOTH EDGES 1 cm, FOLDING TWICE, SEW WITH MACHINE TO STEADY

⑦ SLEEVE
1.5 cm
HAND-STITCH
1 cm
(WRONG SIDE)
1 cm
MACHINE STITCH
GATHER, SEW ON BODY

⑧ BODICE
BACK
FRONT
TURN IN EDGES
WHIP-STITCH

NECKLINE & FRONT LACE
FOLD LACE IN HALF
HAND-STITCH
FOLD
MAKE 40 cm LACE INTO 12 cm BY DRAWING THREAD
SEW AROUND THE NECK AND CENTER FRONT
3.5 cm
1

⑩ HAIR
(STRANDS OF EMBROIDERY COTTON)
25 cm
FOLDS
3 BUNDLES
36 STRANDS OF 4 cm FRONT HAIR
FOLDS
FASTEN WITH 1 STRAND
FRONT
5 cm
BACK
SECURE
TURN UP

CHIGNON
150 cm
TWIST
WIND 3 BUNDLES INTO SKEIN
FOLD IN HALF, TWIST TOGETHER
65 cm
FOLDS
FOLDS
4 cm
WIND
TURN IN ENDS
GLUE ON BACK
SECURE FIRMLY

RIBBON
FINISH 60 cm LONG RIBBON IN A BOWKNOT
SEW ON 2 PIECES
70 cm LONG
80 cm LONG

HAIR ORNAMENT
ATTACH FLOWERS
PUT RIBBON HERE

FINISHED DIAGRAM
GLUE SLEEVE END TO HAND
2 cm
GLUE SLEEVE ENDS TOGETHER
42 cm
PUT FLOWER ON RIBBON
ACCESSORY FOR THE SKIRT LACE RIBBON
7 cm
GATHER
30 cm LONG

ROYAL PRINCESS OF THE STARS

Shown on page 40.

If a star-print fabric is not available, make her the princess of your own choice, such as apples, flowers, or birds. Make her face somewhat smaller than its size.

YOU'LL NEED:
Head-Foundation, Body, Arms, Legs—70 cm by 28 cm white rayon. Face, Nose, Arms, Legs—50 cm by 28 cm cotton jersey. Eyes—dacron georgette. Mouth—strands of embroidery thread. Hair—strands of embroidery thread, 13 cm of 2.5 cm broadcloth. Bloomer, Petticoat—85 cm by 26 cm white georgette. Dress, Veil—90 cm by 85 cm dacron print, 72 cm by 37 cm silver lamé, 62 cm of 2.5 cm braid. Also—packing, cotton wadding, polyester batting.
FINISHED SIZE: Refer to diagram.

INSTRUCTIONS:
Make by referring to Hiji on pages 50-64 for basic method.
Stuff polyester batting firmly into arms and legs. Before the bodice is sewn on, lay wadding thinly over the body. Make collar by gathering braid and stitch to position.
Put silver lamé on wrong side of veil, securing with slip-stitch.
Sew on hair, put veil over, secure with slip-stitch. Put crown on top.

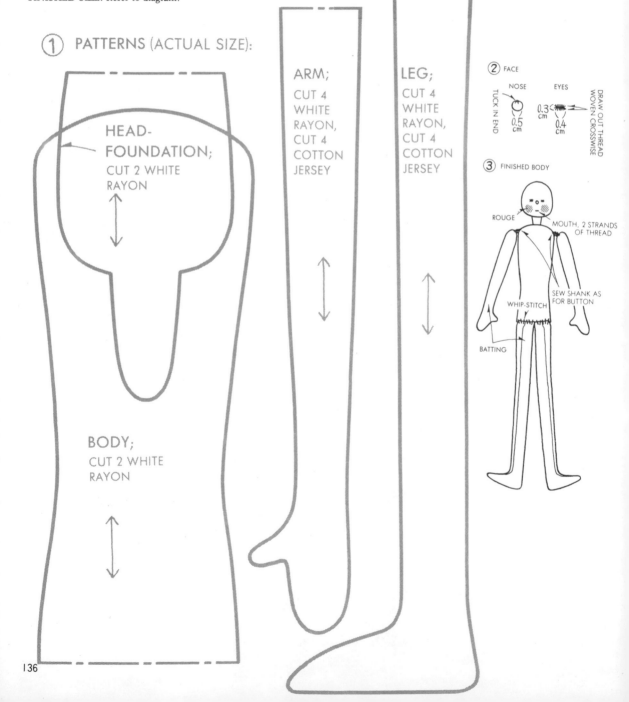

① PATTERNS (ACTUAL SIZE):

HEAD-FOUNDATION;
CUT 2 WHITE RAYON

BODY;
CUT 2 WHITE RAYON

ARM;
CUT 4 WHITE RAYON,
CUT 4 COTTON JERSEY

LEG;
CUT 4 WHITE RAYON,
CUT 4 COTTON JERSEY

② FACE
TUCK IN END
NOSE
0.5 cm
EYES
0.3 cm
0.4 cm
DRAW OUT THREAD WOVEN CROSSWISE

③ FINISHED BODY
ROUGE
MOUTH, 2 STRANDS OF THREAD
SEW SHANK AS FOR BUTTON
WHIP-STITCH
BATTING

DRESS, VEIL, UNDERWEAR

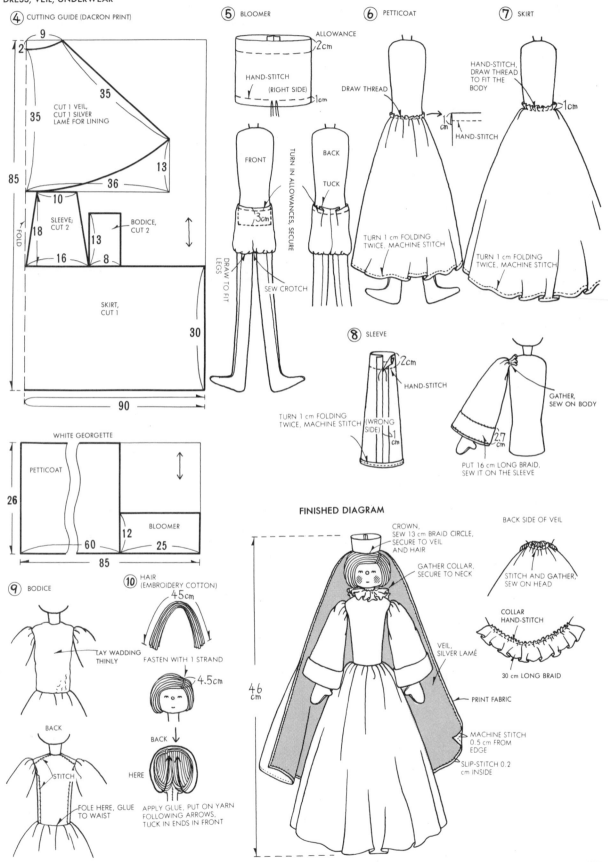

④ CUTTING GUIDE (DACRON PRINT)

9
2
35
35
13
36
CUT 1 VEIL,
CUT 1 SILVER
LAMÉ FOR LINING

85
FOLD

10
SLEEVE;
CUT 2
18
13
16
8
BODICE,
CUT 2

SKIRT,
CUT 1

30

90

WHITE GEORGETTE

PETTICOAT

26

60
12
BLOOMER
25

85

⑤ BLOOMER

ALLOWANCE
2cm
HAND-STITCH
(RIGHT SIDE)
1cm

FRONT
BACK
TUCK

TURN IN ALLOWANCES, SECURE

3cm

DRAW TO FIT LEGS
SEW CROTCH

⑥ PETTICOAT

DRAW THREAD
1cm
HAND-STITCH
TURN 1 cm FOLDING
TWICE, MACHINE STITCH

⑦ SKIRT

HAND-STITCH,
DRAW THREAD
TO FIT THE
BODY
1cm
TURN 1 cm FOLDING
TWICE, MACHINE STITCH

⑧ SLEEVE

2cm
HAND-STITCH
TURN 1 cm FOLDING
TWICE, MACHINE STITCH (WRONG SIDE)
1 cm

GATHER,
SEW ON BODY
2.7 cm
PUT 16 cm LONG BRAID,
SEW IT ON THE SLEEVE

FINISHED DIAGRAM

CROWN,
SEW 13 cm BRAID CIRCLE,
SECURE TO VEIL
AND HAIR

GATHER COLLAR,
SECURE TO NECK

VEIL,
SILVER LAMÉ

PRINT FABRIC

MACHINE STITCH
0.5 cm FROM
EDGE

SLIP-STITCH 0.2
cm INSIDE

46 cm

BACK SIDE OF VEIL

STITCH AND GATHER,
SEW ON HEAD

COLLAR
HAND-STITCH

30 cm LONG BRAID

⑨ BODICE

LAY WADDING
THINLY

BACK

STITCH

FOLE HERE, GLUE
TO WAIST

⑩ HAIR
(EMBROIDERY COTTON)
45cm

FASTEN WITH 1 STRAND
4.5cm

BACK

HERE

APPLY GLUE, PUT ON YARN
FOLLOWING ARROWS,
TUCK IN ENDS IN FRONT

MADAM LILAS

Shown on page 41.

Stuff packing in carefully to give a smooth finish to the front part of the neck. Note the level of chignon in back. Finish the hair and dress in shades of lilac.

① PATTERNS (ACTUAL SIZE):

HEAD-FOUNDATION; CUT 2 WHITE RAYON

LEG; CUT 4 WHITE RAYON, CUT 4 COTTON JERSEY

TURN HERE

ARM; CUT 4 WHITE RAYON, CUT 4 COTTON JERSEY

BODY; CUT 2 WHITE RAYON

YOU'LL NEED:
Head-Foundation, Body, Arms, Legs—78 cm by 29 cm white rayon. Face, Nose, Body, Legs—80 cm by 29 cm cotton jersey. Eyes—dacron georgette. Mouth—strands of embroidery thread. Hair—lightweight yarn. Bloomer, Petticoat—70 cm by 27 cm white broadcloth, 44 cm of 1.5 cm lace. Dress—90 cm by 94 cm cotton print. Also—packing, cotton wadding, polyester batting.
FINISHED SIZE: Refer to diagram.
INSTRUCTIONS:
Make by referring to directions for Hiji on pages 50-64. Finish arms and legs firmly with polyster batting.
Use selvages of fabric for the ruffles on skirt and bodice. Sew on bodice up to arm pit.
Sew on hair following arrows as shown, make chignon on back, secure firmly.

② FACE

NOSE

EYES

TUCK IN EDGES

0.4 cm

0.2 cm

0.4 cm

DRAW OUT THREADS WOVEN CROSSWISE

③ FINISHED BODY

ROUGE

DRAW OUT THREADS WOVEN CROSSWISE

SEW SHANK AS FOR BUTTON

BATTING

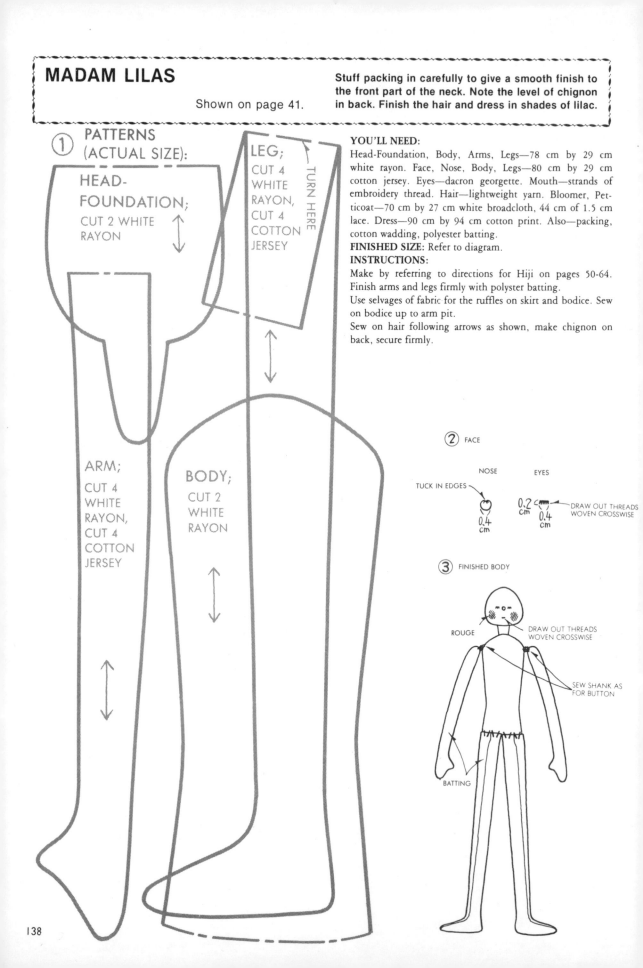

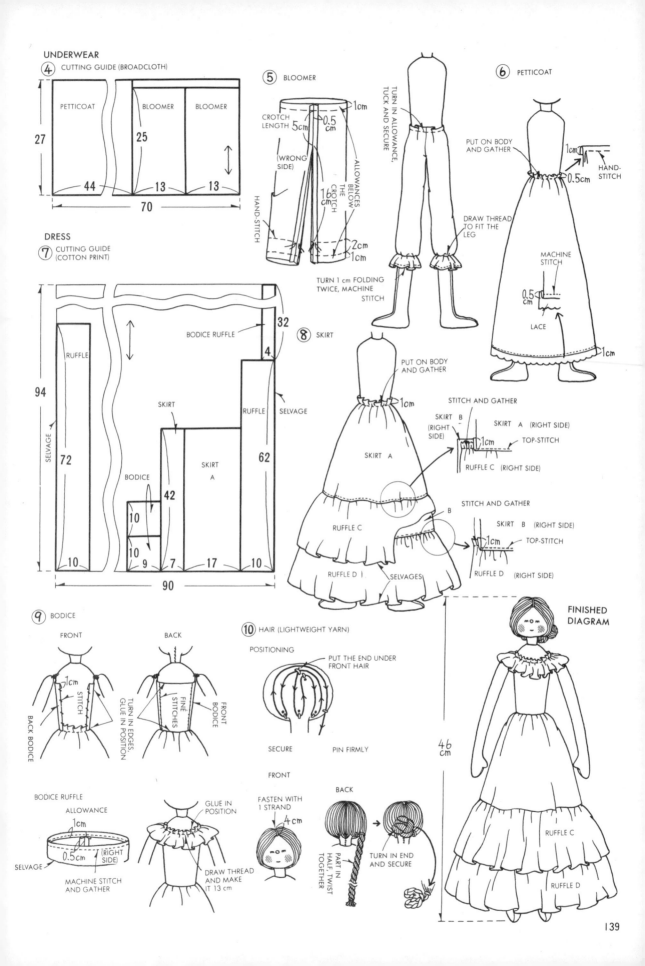

UNDERWEAR

④ CUTTING GUIDE (BROADCLOTH)

PETTICOAT 27
44
BLOOMER 25
13
BLOOMER
13
70

⑤ BLOOMER

1cm
CROTCH LENGTH 5cm
0.5 cm
(WRONG SIDE)
ALLOWANCES BELOW THE CROTCH 16cm
HAND-STITCH
2cm
1cm

TURN 1 cm FOLDING TWICE, MACHINE STITCH

TURN IN ALLOWANCE, TUCK AND SECURE

DRAW THREAD TO FIT THE LEG

⑥ PETTICOAT

PUT ON BODY AND GATHER
1cm
0.5cm
HAND-STITCH
MACHINE STITCH
0.5 cm
LACE
1cm

DRESS

⑦ CUTTING GUIDE (COTTON PRINT)

0.5cm
BODICE RUFFLE
32
4
RUFFLE 72
SELVAGE
94
SKIRT
RUFFLE 62
SELVAGE
BODICE
42
SKIRT A
10
10
9
7
17
10
10
90

⑧ SKIRT

PUT ON BODY AND GATHER
1cm
SKIRT A
RUFFLE C
RUFFLE D
SELVAGES

STITCH AND GATHER
SKIRT B (RIGHT SIDE)
SKIRT A (RIGHT SIDE)
1cm
TOP-STITCH
RUFFLE C (RIGHT SIDE)

STITCH AND GATHER
B
SKIRT B (RIGHT SIDE)
1cm
TOP-STITCH
RUFFLE D (RIGHT SIDE)

⑨ BODICE

FRONT
BACK
1cm
STITCH
BACK BODICE
TURN IN EDGES, GLUE IN POSITION
FINE STITCHES
FRONT BODICE

BODICE RUFFLE
ALLOWANCE
1cm
0.5cm
(RIGHT SIDE)
SELVAGE
MACHINE STITCH AND GATHER

GLUE IN POSITION
DRAW THREAD AND MAKE IT 13 cm

⑩ HAIR (LIGHTWEIGHT YARN)

POSITIONING
PUT THE END UNDER FRONT HAIR

SECURE
PIN FIRMLY

FRONT
FASTEN WITH 1 STRAND
4cm

BACK
PART IN HALF, TWIST TOGETHER
TURN IN END AND SECURE

FINISHED DIAGRAM
46 cm
RUFFLE C
RUFFLE D

139

JOHN & BARBARA

Shown on page 42.

The twins are made in the same way. Simply make one a boy and the other a girl, disigning their face and legs differently. Make dresses with a soft fabric in a pale color.

YOU'LL NEED:
Head-Foundation, Body, Arms, Legs—45 cm by 23 cm white rayon. Face, Nose, Arms, Legs—40 cm by 20 cm beige cotton jersey. Eyes—dacron georgette. Mouth—strands of embroidery thread. Hair—mohair yarn. Dress, Cap, Bloomer—40 cm by 26 cm crepe, 40 cm of 0.6 cm ribbon, 50 cm of 2.5 cm lace. Also—packing, cotton wadding, polyster batting.

FINISHED SIZE: Refer to diagram.
INSTRUCTIONS:
Make according to the directions for Hiji shown on pages 50-64. Make hair, winding yarn round fingers, and sew all over head without snipping the yarn between curls.

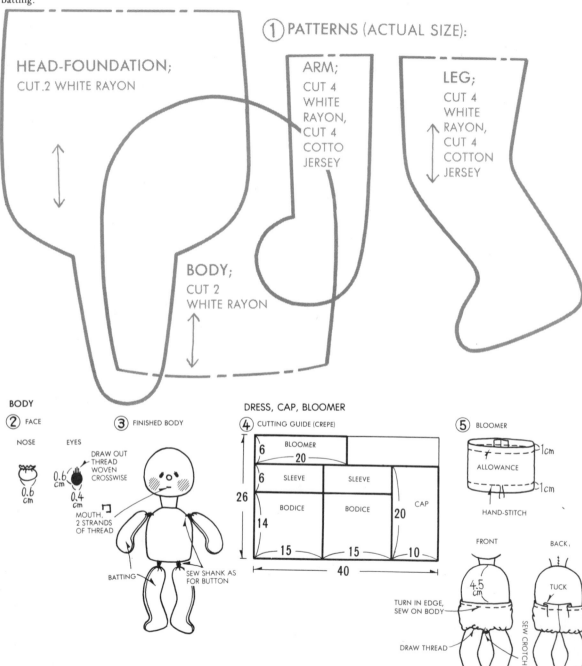

① PATTERNS (ACTUAL SIZE):

HEAD-FOUNDATION;
CUT 2 WHITE RAYON

ARM;
CUT 4 WHITE RAYON, CUT 4 COTTO JERSEY

LEG;
CUT 4 WHITE RAYON, CUT 4 COTTON JERSEY

BODY;
CUT 2 WHITE RAYON

BODY
② FACE
NOSE
EYES
0.6 cm
0.6 cm
0.4 cm
DRAW OUT THREAD WOVEN CROSSWISE
MOUTH, 2 STRANDS OF THREAD

③ FINISHED BODY
BATTING
SEW SHANK AS FOR BUTTON

DRESS, CAP, BLOOMER
④ CUTTING GUIDE (CREPE)
BLOOMER 20
6
6 SLEEVE — SLEEVE
26
BODICE — BODICE — 20 — CAP
14
15 — 15 — 10
40

⑤ BLOOMER
1cm
ALLOWANCE
1cm
HAND-STITCH

FRONT
4.5 cm
BACK
TUCK
TURN IN EDGE, SEW ON BODY
DRAW THREAD
SEW CROTCH

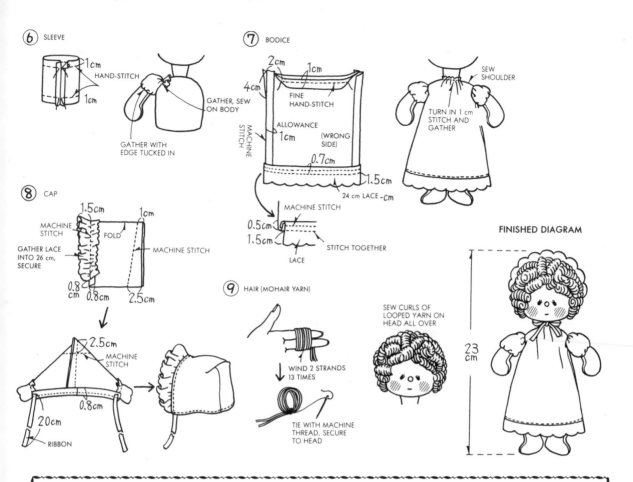

⑥ SLEEVE

1cm
HAND-STITCH
1cm

GATHER WITH
EDGE TUCKED IN

GATHER, SEW
ON BODY

⑦ BODICE

2cm
1cm
4cm
FINE HAND-STITCH
MACHINE STITCH
ALLOWANCE
1cm
(WRONG SIDE)
0.7cm
1.5cm
24 cm LACE -cm

SEW SHOULDER

TURN IN 1 cm
STITCH AND
GATHER

MACHINE STITCH
0.5cm
1.5cm
STITCH TOGETHER
LACE

⑧ CAP

1.5cm
1cm
MACHINE STITCH
FOLD
MACHINE STITCH
GATHER LACE INTO 26 cm, SECURE
0.8 cm
0.8cm
2.5cm

2.5cm
MACHINE STITCH
0.8cm
20cm
RIBBON

⑨ HAIR (MOHAIR YARN)

WIND 2 STRANDS 13 TIMES

TIE WITH MACHINE THREAD, SECURE TO HEAD

FINISHED DIAGRAM

SEW CURLS OF LOOPED YARN ON HEAD ALL OVER

23 cm

MIMI & LULU & POPO

Shown on page 43.

Make these all in the same manner, using an easy-to-handle sheer fabric like lawn. Mark the different individuals with their dresses.

YOU'LL NEED (for each):
Head-Foundation, Body, Arms, Legs—40 cm by 27 cm white rayon. Face, Nose, Arms, Legs—50 cm by 15 cm beige georgette. Eyes—dacron georgette. Mouth—strands of embroidery thread. Hair—frizzle yarn, 20 cm of 0.3 cm ribbon. Bloomer—20 cm by 10 cm white broadcloth. Petticoat—60 cm of 5 cm lace. Dress, Cap—50 cm by 25.5 cm lawn, 28 cm of 1.5 cm lace. Also—packing, cotton wadding, polyester batting.
FINISHED SIZE: Refer to diagram.
INSTRUCTIONS:
Make according to the method on pages 50-64.
Sew on hair in same manner as shown on page 72.
Make each in the same way and clothe in dresses of different color.

① PATTERNS (ACTUAL SIZE):

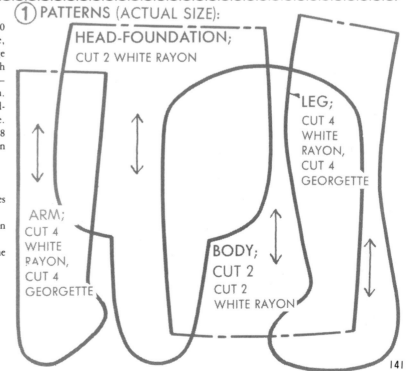

HEAD-FOUNDATION;
CUT 2 WHITE RAYON

LEG;
CUT 4 WHITE RAYON,
CUT 4 GEORGETTE

ARM;
CUT 4 WHITE RAYON,
CUT 4 GEORGETTE

BODY;
CUT 2
CUT 2 WHITE RAYON

② FACE

NOSE
0.4 cm

EYES
0.5 cm
0.3 cm
DRAW OUT THREAD WOVEN CROSSWISE

③ FINISHED BODY

ROUGE
MOUTH, 6 STRANDS OF THREAD
SEW SHANK AS FOR BUTTON
BATING

④ BLOOMER (BROADCLOTH)

CUT 2
10
10

FRONT
5cm
TURN IN 1 cm, SEW ON BODY

BACK
TUCK

DRAW THREAD TO FIT THE LEG

ALLOWANCE
1cm
CROTCH LENGTH
3cm
BELOW THE CROTCH
5cm
HAND-STITCH
1cm

⑤ PETTICOAT (LACE)

LAY 2 PIECES OF LACE AND STITCH
5cm
5cm
3cm
30cm

STITCH AND GATHER
0.5cm

DRESS, CAP

⑥ CUTTING GUIDE

	14		BODICE			
5	SLEEVE					
5	SLEEVE		8	8		CAP
25.5						
11	SKIRT				8.5	9.5	8.5
	30				9	9
4.5	RIBBON					
	50					

⑦ SLEEVE

HAND-STITCH
1cm
0.8 cm
1cm

GATHER ON BODY, SEW
DRAW THREAD, TUCK IN DEGE

⑧ SKIRT

SEW ON BODY
1cm
TURN 1 cm FOLDING TWICE, SLIP-STITCH

⑨ BODICE

FRONT
STITCH SHOULDERS AND SIDES
RIBBON

BACK
FINISH IN BOW KNOT
CUT OFF
TURN 1 cm FOLD TWICE, MACHINE STITCH

FINISHED DIAGRAM
GLUE CAP TO HEAD
25 cm

⑩ HAIR (FRIZZLE YARN)

200 STRANDS OF 32 cm YARN, FASTEN AT THE CENTER
BRAID 24 STRANDS
16cm
TRIM FRONT
RIBBON

⑪ CAP

LACE
1cm
1cm
(WRONG SIDE)
TURN 1 cm FOLDING TWICE, MACHINE STITCH

PRINCESS FROM THE LAND OF BAMBOO

Shown on page 44.

These are very simply made. Make them stand by putting a felt piece over the cardboard base. Make the grandparents' features by referring to the picture.

YOU'LL NEED (for each):

Head-Foundation—9 cm by 15 cm white rayon. Face, Nose —20 cm by 20 cm beige georgette. Eyes—dacron georgette. Mouth—strands of embroidery thread. Body—6.5 cm by 13 cm cardboard. Also—packing, cotton wadding, polyester batting.

(Princess): Kimono—17 cm by 6.5 cm each, light pink, rose felt. Collar—17 cm by 3 cm each, white, purple felt. Hair—sport-weight yarn. Ribbon—strands of cotton small amount each, yellow brown, pink.

(Grandma): Kimono—6.5 cm by 17 cm dark blue felt. Collar—17 cm by 3 cm each, white, gray felt. Wrinkles— silk thread. Hair—worsted-weight yarn.

(Grandpa): Kimono—6.5 cm by 17 cm dark green felt. Collar—17 cm by 3 cm each, white, brown felt. Wrinkles— silk thread. Hair—worsted-weight yarn.

FINISHED SIZE: Refer to diagram.

INSTRUCTIONS:

Make heads and faces according to directions for Hiji on pages 50-64. Make grandpa's face long lengthwise. Put a little rounded wadding on the faces of both grandparents right above the mouths. Draw the thread of sewn wrinkles to make their facial features.

1 PATTERNS (ACTUAL SIZE):

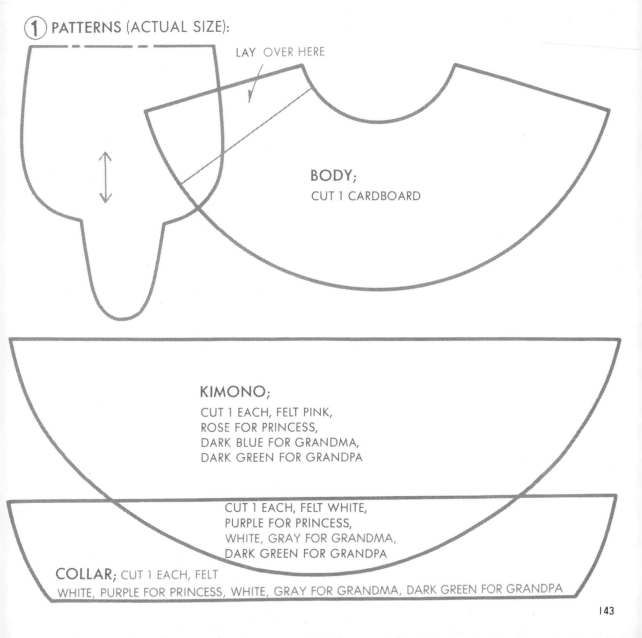

LAY OVER HERE

BODY;
CUT 1 CARDBOARD

KIMONO;
CUT 1 EACH, FELT PINK,
ROSE FOR PRINCESS,
DARK BLUE FOR GRANDMA,
DARK GREEN FOR GRANDPA

CUT 1 EACH, FELT WHITE,
PURPLE FOR PRINCESS,
WHITE, GRAY FOR GRANDMA,
DARK GREEN FOR GRANDPA

COLLAR; CUT 1 EACH, FELT
WHITE, PURPLE FOR PRINCESS, WHITE, GRAY FOR GRANDMA, DARK GREEN FOR GRANDPA

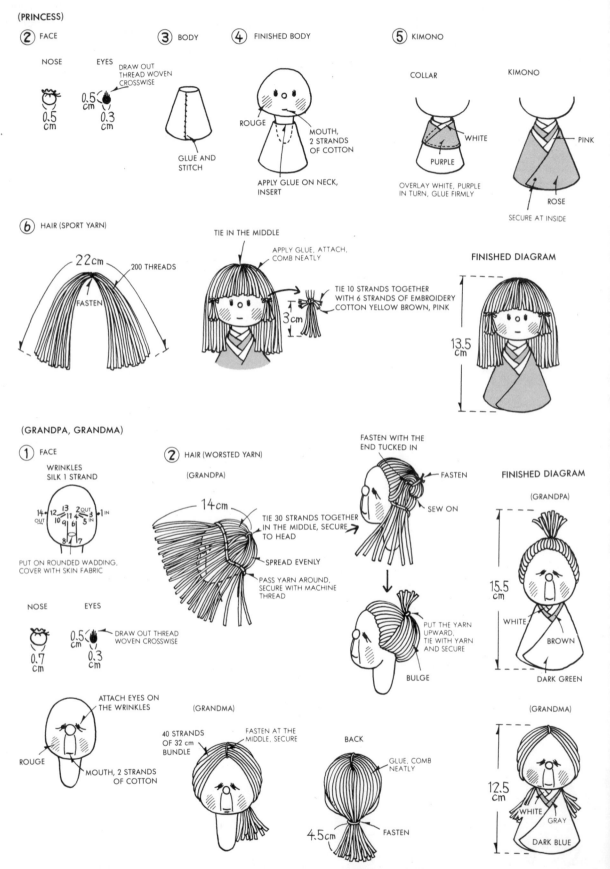

(PRINCESS)

2 FACE

NOSE

EYES

DRAW OUT THREAD WOVEN CROSSWISE

0.5 cm

0.5 cm   0.3 cm

3 BODY

GLUE AND STITCH

4 FINISHED BODY

ROUGE

MOUTH, 2 STRANDS OF COTTON

APPLY GLUE ON NECK, INSERT

5 KIMONO

COLLAR

WHITE

PURPLE

OVERLAY WHITE, PURPLE IN TURN, GLUE FIRMLY

KIMONO

PINK

ROSE

SECURE AT INSIDE

6 HAIR (SPORT YARN)

22cm   200 THREADS

FASTEN

TIE IN THE MIDDLE

APPLY GLUE, ATTACH, COMB NEATLY

TIE 10 STRANDS TOGETHER WITH 6 STRANDS OF EMBROIDERY COTTON YELLOW BROWN, PINK

3 cm

FINISHED DIAGRAM

13.5 cm

(GRANDPA, GRANDMA)

1 FACE

WRINKLES SILK 1 STRAND

14 OUT · 12 13 · 2 OUT · 1 IN
10 9 11 4 3 IN
8 7 6 5

PUT ON ROUNDED WADDING, COVER WITH SKIN FABRIC

NOSE

EYES

DRAW OUT THREAD WOVEN CROSSWISE

0.7 cm   0.5 cm   0.3 cm

ATTACH EYES ON THE WRINKLES

ROUGE

MOUTH, 2 STRANDS OF COTTON

2 HAIR (WORSTED YARN)

(GRANDPA)

14cm

TIE 30 STRANDS TOGETHER IN THE MIDDLE, SECURE TO HEAD

SPREAD EVENLY

PASS YARN AROUND, SECURE WITH MACHINE THREAD

FASTEN WITH THE END TUCKED IN

FASTEN

SEW ON

PUT THE YARN UPWARD, TIE WITH YARN AND SECURE

BULGE

(GRANDMA)

40 STRANDS OF 32 cm BUNDLE

FASTEN AT THE MIDDLE, SECURE

BACK

GLUE, COMB NEATLY

4.5cm   FASTEN

FINISHED DIAGRAM

(GRANDPA)

15.5 cm

WHITE

BROWN

DARK GREEN

(GRANDMA)

12.5 cm

WHITE   GRAY

DARK BLUE

144

GLOWING SUNSET

Shown on page 45.

Noses are very tiny, as you see in the picture. Attach skin fabric cut to nose size in its position. For fabric, try to use one of most Japaneselike patterns.

YOU'LL NEED (for each):

Head-Foundation—8 cm by 12 cm white rayon. Body, Collar —14 cm by 9 cm cotton fabric. Face, Nose—10 cm by 10 cm beige georgette. Eyes—dacron georgette. Mouth—strands of embroidery thread. Hair—sport-weight yarn. Also—packing, cotton wadding, polyester batting.

FINISHED SIZE: Refer to diagram.

INSTRUCTIONS:

Make by referring to pages 50-64 for the basic method.
Seam body along the pattern and cut out, leaving a little allowance all around; turn right side out and stuff packing firmly.

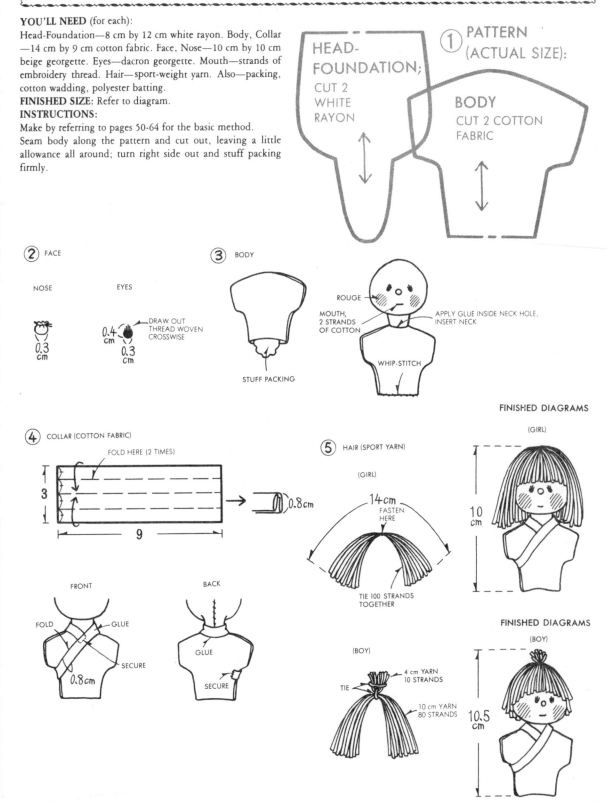

① PATTERN (ACTUAL SIZE):

HEAD-FOUNDATION; CUT 2 WHITE RAYON

BODY CUT 2 COTTON FABRIC

② FACE

NOSE

0.3 cm

EYES

0.4 cm

DRAW OUT THREAD WOVEN CROSSWISE

0.3 cm

③ BODY

STUFF PACKING

ROUGE

MOUTH, 2 STRANDS OF COTTON

APPLY GLUE INSIDE NECK HOLE, INSERT NECK

WHIP-STITCH

④ COLLAR (COTTON FABRIC)

FOLD HERE (2 TIMES)

3

9

0.8cm

FRONT

FOLD

GLUE

SECURE

0.8cm

BACK

GLUE

SECURE

⑤ HAIR (SPORT YARN)

(GIRL)

14cm FASTEN HERE

TIE 100 STRANDS TOGETHER

(BOY)

TIE

4 cm YARN 10 STRANDS

10 cm YARN 80 STRANDS

FINISHED DIAGRAMS

(GIRL)

10 cm

FINISHED DIAGRAMS

(BOY)

10.5 cm

145

MITCHI

Shown on page 46.

Though she is very tall, she is very simple to make. Her voluminous skirt is designed to keep things indide, so secure the waist firmly to the body.

YOU'LL NEED:
Head-Foundation, Body, Arms—50 cm by 40 cm white rayon. Face, Noes, Arms—45 cm by 30 cm cotton jersey. Body—34 cm by 16 cm corduroy. Eyes—dacron georgette. Mouth—strands of embroidery thread. Hair—lightweight yarn. Sleeves, Skirt, Hood—90 cm by 80 cm velveteen, 90 cm of 3 cm lace, 80 cm of 0.7 cm velvet ribbon. In-Pocket—

90 cm by 47 cm white rayon. Also—packing, cotton wadding, polyester batting.
FINISHED SIZE: Refer to diagram.
INSTRUCTIONS:
Make by referring to pages 54-64 for the basic method. Machine stitch the corduroy body laid over the white rayon. Sew pocket on the skirt, make an opening at center back.

1 PATTERNS (ACTUAL SIZE):

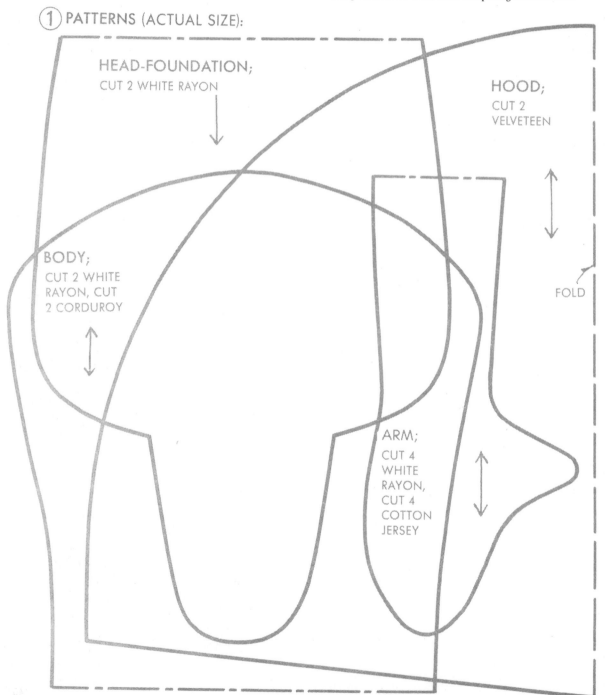

HEAD-FOUNDATION;
CUT 2 WHITE RAYON

HOOD;
CUT 2
VELVETEEN

FOLD

BODY;
CUT 2 WHITE
RAYON, CUT
2 CORDUROY

ARM;
CUT 4
WHITE
RAYON,
CUT 4
COTTON
JERSEY

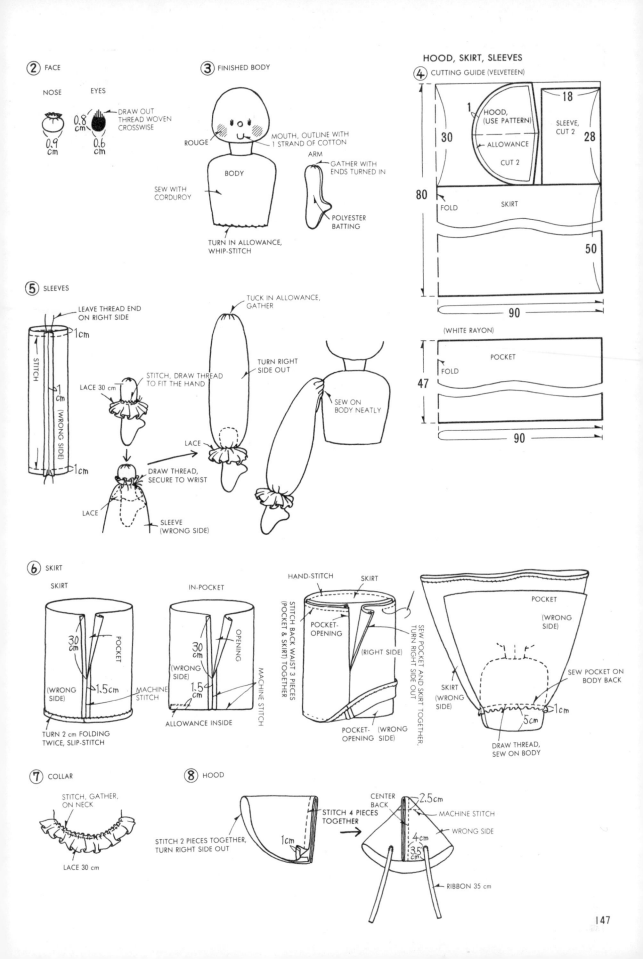

② FACE

NOSE

EYES

0.9 cm

0.8 cm

0.6 cm

DRAW OUT THREAD WOVEN CROSSWISE

③ FINISHED BODY

ROUGE

MOUTH, OUTLINE WITH 1 STRAND OF COTTON

ARM

GATHER WITH ENDS TURNED IN

BODY

SEW WITH CORDUROY

POLYESTER BATTING

TURN IN ALLOWANCE, WHIP-STITCH

HOOD, SKIRT, SLEEVES

④ CUTTING GUIDE (VELVETEEN)

1

HOOD, (USE PATTERN)

18

SLEEVE, CUT 2

30

ALLOWANCE

CUT 2

28

80

FOLD

SKIRT

50

90

(WHITE RAYON)

POCKET

FOLD

47

90

⑤ SLEEVES

LEAVE THREAD END ON RIGHT SIDE

1cm

STITCH

1 cm

(WRONG SIDE)

1cm

LACE 30 cm

STITCH, DRAW THREAD TO FIT THE HAND

TUCK IN ALLOWANCE, GATHER

TURN RIGHT SIDE OUT

SEW ON BODY NEATLY

LACE

DRAW THREAD, SECURE TO WRIST

LACE

SLEEVE (WRONG SIDE)

⑥ SKIRT

SKIRT

IN-POCKET

HAND-STITCH

SKIRT

30 cm

POCKET

30 cm

OPENING

STITCH BACK WAIST 3 PIECES (POCKET & SKIRT) TOGETHER

POCKET

(WRONG SIDE)

(WRONG SIDE)

(WRONG SIDE)

1.5cm

MACHINE STITCH

1.5 cm

MACHINE STITCH

POCKET-OPENING

(RIGHT SIDE)

SEW POCKET AND SKIRT TOGETHER. TURN RIGHT SIDE OUT.

SEW POCKET ON BODY BACK

TURN 2 cm FOLDING TWICE, SLIP-STITCH

ALLOWANCE INSIDE

POCKET-OPENING

(WRONG SIDE)

SKIRT (WRONG SIDE)

5cm

1cm

DRAW THREAD, SEW ON BODY

⑦ COLLAR

STITCH, GATHER, ON NECK

LACE 30 cm

⑧ HOOD

STITCH 2 PIECES TOGETHER, TURN RIGHT SIDE OUT

1cm

CENTER BACK

STITCH 4 PIECES TOGETHER

2.5cm

MACHINE STITCH

WRONG SIDE

4 cm

3.5cm

RIBBON 35 cm

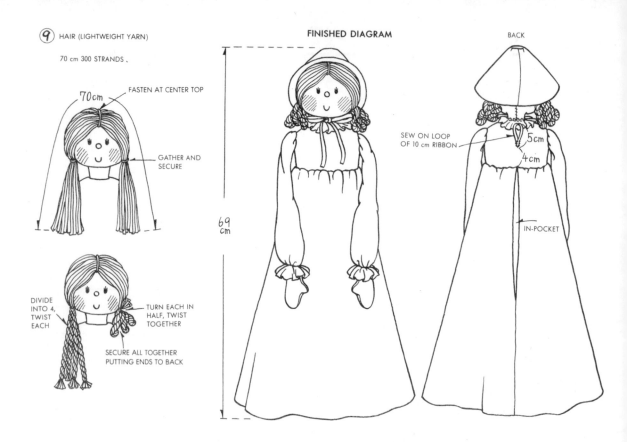

⑨ HAIR (LIGHTWEIGHT YARN)

70 cm 300 STRANDS

70cm — FASTEN AT CENTER TOP

GATHER AND SECURE

FINISHED DIAGRAM

69 cm

BACK

SEW ON LOOP OF 10 cm RIBBON

5cm

4cm

IN-POCKET

DIVIDE INTO 4, TWIST EACH

TURN EACH IN HALF, TWIST TOGETHER

SECURE ALL TOGETHER PUTTING ENDS TO BACK

ROMMY & DORON

Shown on page 47.

Those are long bodied dolls with short legs. Stuff the body carefully to give a smooth finish. Make them marionettes, and enjoy talking and manipulating them.

YOU'LL NEED:

(**Rommy**): Head-Foundation, Arms, Legs—76 cm by 26 cm white rayon. Face, Nose, Arms, Legs—66 cm by 26 cm beige cotton jersey. Eyes—dacron georgette. Mouth—strands of embroidery thread. Hair—pink, blue, worsted yarn, No. 30 wire taped green. Body, Arm, Dress—88 cm by 56 cm veleteen print, 100 cm of 1.5 cm lace. Shoes—36 cm by 16 cm navy blue velveteen, 14 cm by 10 cm purple felt. Also—pearl cotton, packing, cotton wadding, polyester batting.

(**Doron**): Head-Foundation, Arms, Legs—76 cm by 26 cm white rayon. Face, Nose, Arms—44 cm by 26 cm beige jersey. Legs—20 cm by 20 cm striped jersey. Eyes—dacron georgette. Mouth—strands of embroidery thread. Hair—

blue, gray worsted yarn. Body, Arms, Dress—90 cm by 43 cm blue gray velveteen, 26 cm of 1.5 cm braid, 22 cm of 2 cm braid, strands of embroidery cotton. Shoes—36 cm by 16 cm brown corduroy, 14 cm by 10 cm dark blue felt. Also —same as Rommy.

INSTRUCTIONS:

Make by referring to pages 50-64 for the basic method. Make nose from a scrap of cotton jersey colored in orange with felt-tip pen.

Body and arms are made of dress fabric.

Sew on marionette strings of pearl cotton cut in desired length.

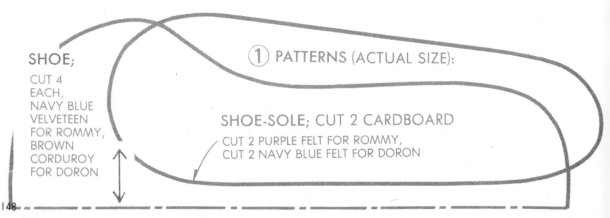

SHOE;

CUT 4 EACH, NAVY BLUE VELVETEEN FOR ROMMY, BROWN CORDUROY FOR DORON

① PATTERNS (ACTUAL SIZE):

SHOE-SOLE; CUT 2 CARDBOARD
CUT 2 PURPLE FELT FOR ROMMY,
CUT 2 NAVY BLUE FELT FOR DORON

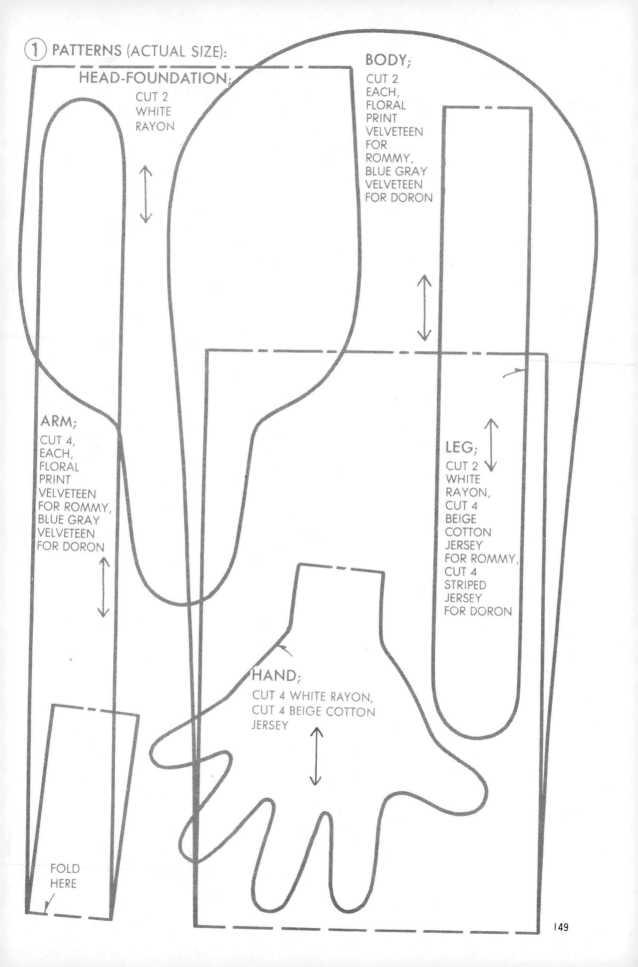

1 PATTERNS (ACTUAL SIZE):

HEAD-FOUNDATION;
CUT 2
WHITE
RAYON

BODY;
CUT 2
EACH,
FLORAL
PRINT
VELVETEEN
FOR
ROMMY,
BLUE GRAY
VELVETEEN
FOR DORON

ARM;
CUT 4,
EACH,
FLORAL
PRINT
VELVETEEN
FOR ROMMY,
BLUE GRAY
VELVETEEN
FOR DORON

LEG;
CUT 2
WHITE
RAYON,
CUT 4
BEIGE
COTTON
JERSEY
FOR ROMMY,
CUT 4
STRIPED
JERSEY
FOR DORON

HAND;
CUT 4 WHITE RAYON,
CUT 4 BEIGE COTTON
JERSEY

FOLD
HERE

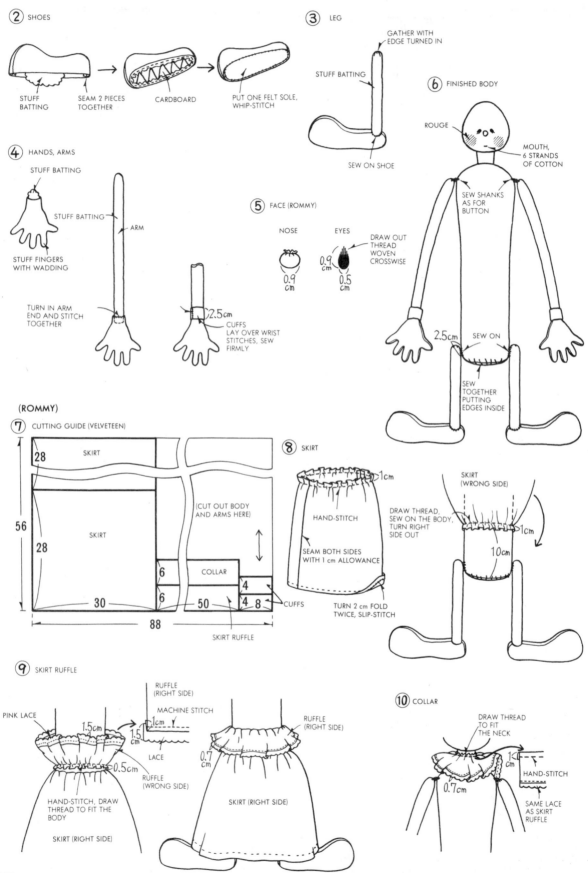

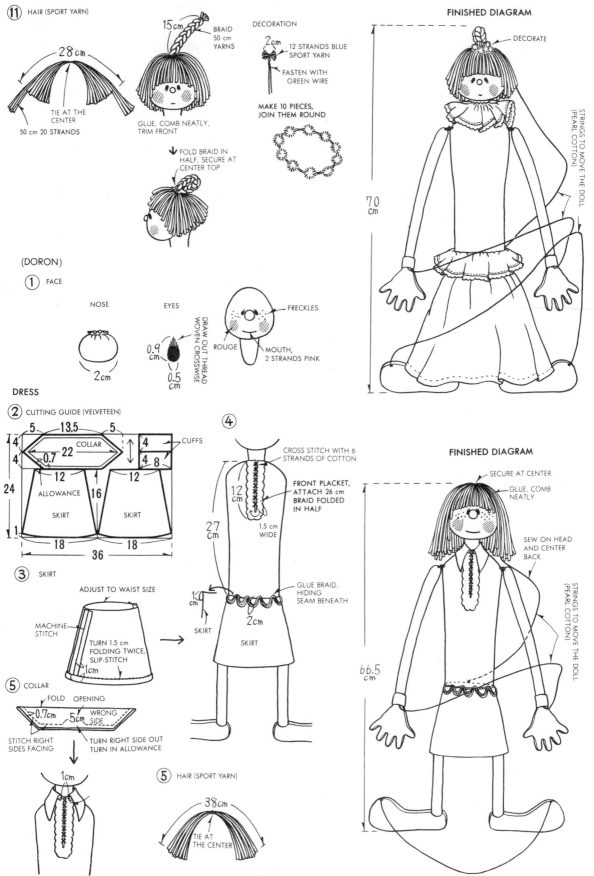

⑪ HAIR (SPORT YARN)

28cm

TIE AT THE CENTER
50 cm 20 STRANDS

15cm — BRAID 50 cm YARNS

GLUE, COMB NEATLY, TRIM FRONT

↓ FOLD BRAID IN HALF, SECURE AT CENTER TOP

DECORATION

2cm — 12 STRANDS BLUE SPORT YARN

→ FASTEN WITH GREEN WIRE

MAKE 10 PIECES, JOIN THEM ROUND

FINISHED DIAGRAM

70 cm

DECORATE

STRINGS TO MOVE THE DOLL (PEARL COTTON)

(DORON)

① FACE

NOSE

2cm

EYES

0.9 cm

0.5 cm

DRAW OUT THREAD WOVEN CROSSWISE

FRECKLES

ROUGE

MOUTH, 2 STRANDS PINK

DRESS

② CUTTING GUIDE (VELVETEEN)

5   13.5   5

4

COLLAR

22

0.7

4

12   16   12

24

ALLOWANCE

SKIRT   SKIRT

1

18   18

36

4   CUFFS

4   8

③ SKIRT

ADJUST TO WAIST SIZE

MACHINE STITCH

TURN 1.5 cm FOLDING TWICE, SLIP-STITCH

1cm

④

CROSS STITCH WITH 6 STRANDS OF COTTON

12 cm

27 cm

FRONT PLACKET, ATTACH 26 cm BRAID FOLDED IN HALF

1.5 cm WIDE

1 cm

SKIRT

2cm

GLUE BRAID, HIDING SEAM BENEATH

SKIRT

⑤ COLLAR

FOLD   OPENING

0.7cm   5cm

WRONG SIDE

STITCH RIGHT SIDES FACING

TURN RIGHT SIDE OUT TURN IN ALLOWANCE

1cm

⑤ HAIR (SPORT YARN)

38cm

TIE AT THE CENTER

FINISHED DIAGRAM

SECURE AT CENTER

GLUE, COMB NEATLY

SEW ON HEAD AND CENTER BACK

STRINGS TO MOVE THE DOLL (PEARL COTTON)

66.5 cm

151

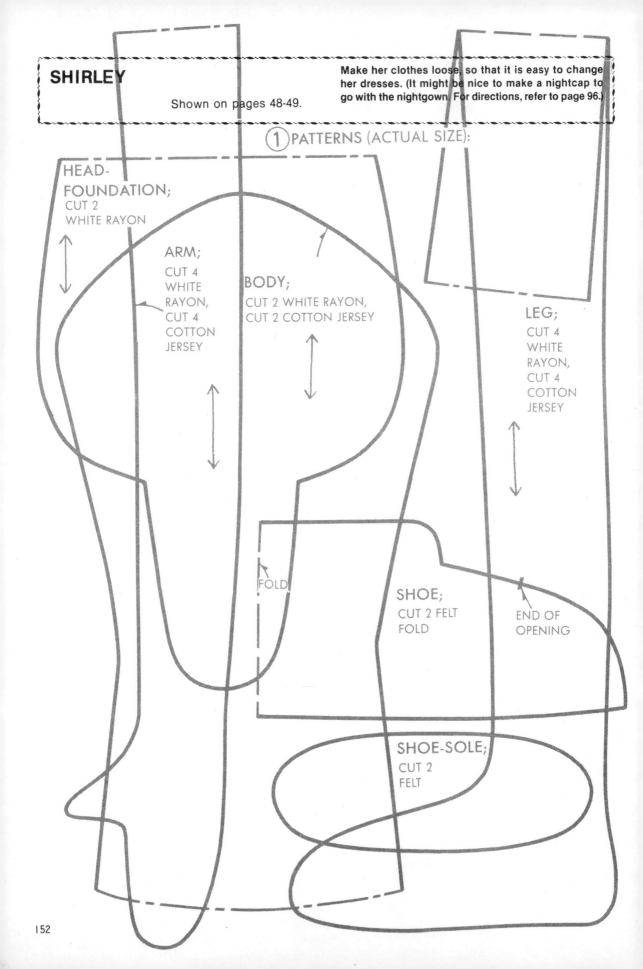

SHIRLEY

Shown on pages 48-49.

Make her clothes loose, so that it is easy to change her dresses. (It might be nice to make a nightcap to go with the nightgown. For directions, refer to page 96.)

① PATTERNS (ACTUAL SIZE):

HEAD-
FOUNDATION;
CUT 2
WHITE RAYON

ARM;
CUT 4
WHITE
RAYON,
CUT 4
COTTON
JERSEY

BODY;
CUT 2 WHITE RAYON,
CUT 2 COTTON JERSEY

LEG;
CUT 4
WHITE
RAYON,
CUT 4
COTTON
JERSEY

FOLD

SHOE;
CUT 2 FELT
FOLD

END OF
OPENING

SHOE-SOLE;
CUT 2
FELT

YOU'LL NEED:

(Body): Head-Foundation, Body, Arms, Legs—90 cm by 56 cm white rayon. Face, Nose, Body, Arms, Legs—52 cm by 81 cm cotton jersey. Eyes—dacron georgette. Mouth—strands of embroidery thread. Hair—worsted-weight yarn.

(Underwear): 70 cm by 40 cm white broadcloth, 80 cm of 2 cm lace, 62 cm of 0.8 cm lace, 2 of 1 cm-diameter button, 10 cm of 0.5 cm elastic.

(Blouse): 90 cm by 37 cm crepe, 10 cm by 10 cm floral lace fabric, 3 of 1 cm-diameter button, 2 pair of small snaps.

(Jumper-skirt); 85 cm by 32 cm wool, 22 cm of 1.5 cm tyrolean tape, 20 cm long zipper fastener.

(Dress): 90 cm by 50 cm cotton print, 10 cm of 2 cm braid, 20 cm long zipper fastener.

(Skirt): 62 cm by 40 cm wool print, 40 cm of 0.5 cm elastic.

(Nightgown); 55 cm by 125 cm cotton border print, 17 cm of 1.3 cm lace, elastic thread, 20 cm long zipper fastener.

(Hat): Raffia yarn, 100 cm of 3.5 cm lace ribbon, artificial flower.

(Shoes): 21 cm by 15 cm felt, 40 cm of 0.3 cm ribbon.

FINISHED SIZE: 62 cm tall.

INSTRUCTIONS:

(Body): Make by referring to pages 50-64 for basic method. Sew on hair in same manner as for Karen on page 72. Finish allowances neatly, since seams are visible when clothes are changed.

(Underwear): Sew pants after the lace is sewn on. Fold back allowances of slip neck and armholes, insert lace and machine stitch.

(Blouse): Sew sleeve to side after sleeve top is joined. Sew lace fabric on front.

(Jumper-skirt): Make 7 pin tucks on front. Finish front neck with tyrolean tape.

(Dress): Finish front neck with its facing. Use selvage for hem ruffle. Pipe end of sleeve, sew underarm.

(Skirt): Make 2 rows of casing on the waist and pass elastic through.

(Nightgown): Make following border print pattern: Decorate front with shirring and finish with lace that is stitched on.

(Hat): Work single crochet firmly with size F hook. Finish with ribbon and flowers.

(Shoes): Join side piece and sole together, using silk thread; pass ribbon through, tie in position.

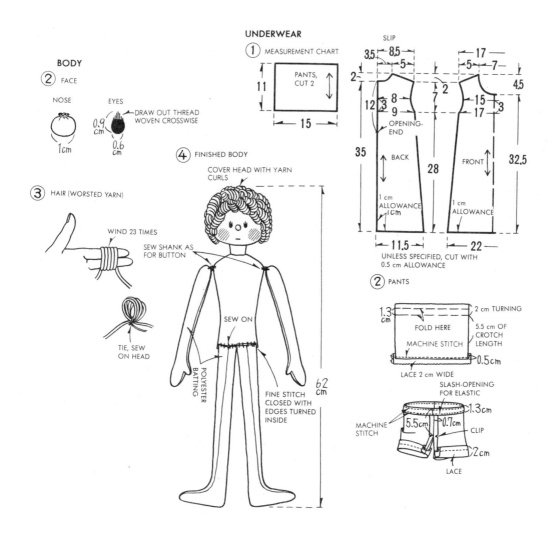

③ SLIP

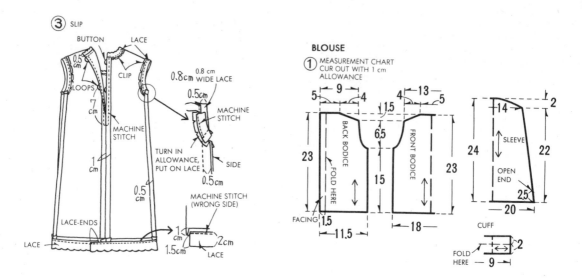

BUTTON · LACE
0.5 cm
CLIP
LOOPS
7 cm
MACHINE STITCH
1 cm
LACE-ENDS
LACE
0.5 cm

0.8 cm WIDE LACE
0.8 cm
0.5 cm
MACHINE STITCH
TURN IN ALLOWANCE, PUT ON LACE
SIDE
0.5 cm

MACHINE STITCH (WRONG SIDE)
1 cm
1.5 cm
2 cm
LACE

BLOUSE

① MEASUREMENT CHART
CUR OUT WITH 1 cm ALLOWANCE

5 · 9 · 4 · 1.5 · 4 · 13 · 5
BACK BODICE · FOLD HERE · 23 · 6.5 · 15 · FRONT BODICE · 23
FACING · 1.5 · 11.5 · 18

14 · 2
SLEEVE · 24 · 22
OPEN END · 2.5
20

CUFF
FOLD HERE · 2
9

② SEWING

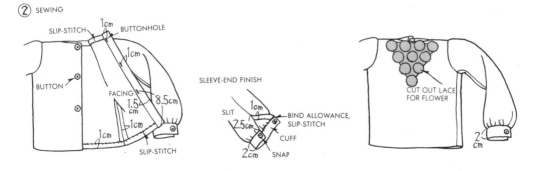

SLIP-STITCH · 1 cm · BUTTONHOLE
1 cm
BUTTON
FACING · 1.5 cm · 8.5 cm
1 cm
1 cm
SLIP-STITCH

SLEEVE-END FINISH
1 cm
SLIT
2.5 cm
2 cm
BIND ALLOWANCE, SLIP-STITCH
CUFF
SNAP

CUT OUT LACE FOR FLOWER
2 cm

JUMPER-SKIRT

① MEASUREMENT CHART

3.5
BACK BODICE CUT 2
DART · 10 · 5 · 5
2.5 · 4 · 1.5
7

2.5 cm FOR PIN-TUCKS INCLUDED
3.5 · 8 · 3.5
FRONT BODICE
6 · 5 · 6
5 · 0.5 cm ALLOWANCE
15

12
BACK SKIRT, CUT 2
10
29 · END OF OPENING
15
2 cm ALLOWANCE

25
FRONT SKIRT
29
31

UNLESS SPECIFIED, CUT WITH 1 cm ALLOWANCE

② SEWING

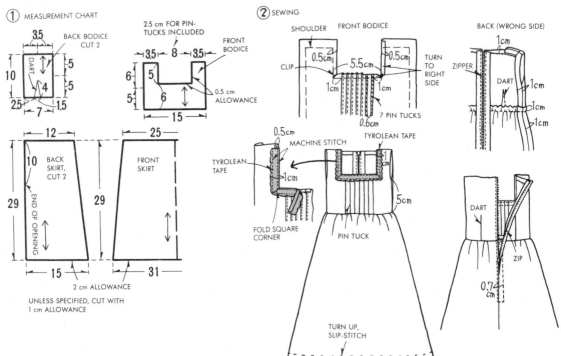

SHOULDER · FRONT BODICE
CLIP · 0.5 cm · 5.5 cm · 0.5 cm
1 cm · 1 cm
TURN TO RIGHT SIDE
7 PIN TUCKS
0.6cm

BACK (WRONG SIDE)
1 cm
ZIPPER · DART · 1 cm
1 cm
1 cm

0.5 cm
MACHINE STITCH
TYROLEAN TAPE
TYROLEAN TAPE
1 cm
FOLD SQUARE CORNER
PIN TUCK
5 cm

DART
ZIP
0.7 cm

TURN UP, SLIP-STITCH

DRESS

① MEASUREMENT CHART

BACK BODICE
CUT 2 FOLDED

5.5
9.5
5
6.5
4.5
6

FRONT BODICE

2.5 5 2.5
6
5
12
3
11

0.5 cm ALLOWANCE

NECK-FACING

2.5 5 2.5
5.5
1
10
2.5

3

SLEEVE,
CUT 2 FOLDED

0.5 cm ALLOWANCE
12
FOLD
1.5
1.5
4
4
4
25

END OF OPENING

SKIRT
FOLD
10.5
24
SLEEVE END
BINDING
60

SKIRT RUFFLE, CUT 2
50
5.5
SELVAGE

13
2
NO ALLOWANCE

UNLESS SPECIFIED, CUT
WITH 1 cm ALLOWANCE

② SEWING

FRONT BODICE

MACHINE
STITCH

BRAID

SEAM WITH FACING,
TOP-STITCH

0.5 cm

FACING

HEM RUFFLE

1cm

SEW 2
PIECES
ROUND

STITCH, DRAW THREAD
TO MAKE IT INTO 60 cm

SELVAGE

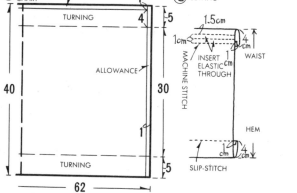

BACK

1cm
20 cm
1 cm
4cm
ZIP
CENTER BACK
(WRONG SIDE)
1cm

SKIRT (RIGHT SIDE)
MACHINE STITCH
1cm
GATHER
1cm
5.5cm

FRONT BODICE

ZIPPER
GATHER
BRAID
0.5 cm
PIPING

SKIRT

① MEASUREMENT CHART

ALLOWANCE
1
TURNING
4
5
ALLOWANCE
40
30
TURNING
5
62

② SEWING

1.5cm
1cm
INSERT ELASTIC THROUGH
MACHINE STITCH
4 cm
1 cm
WAIST
HEM
1
1 cm
4 cm
SLIP-STITCH

INSERT
20 cm ELASTIC
3.5 cm
26.5 cm

155

NIGHTGOWN

UNLESS SPECIFIED, CUT WITH 1 cm ALLOWANCE

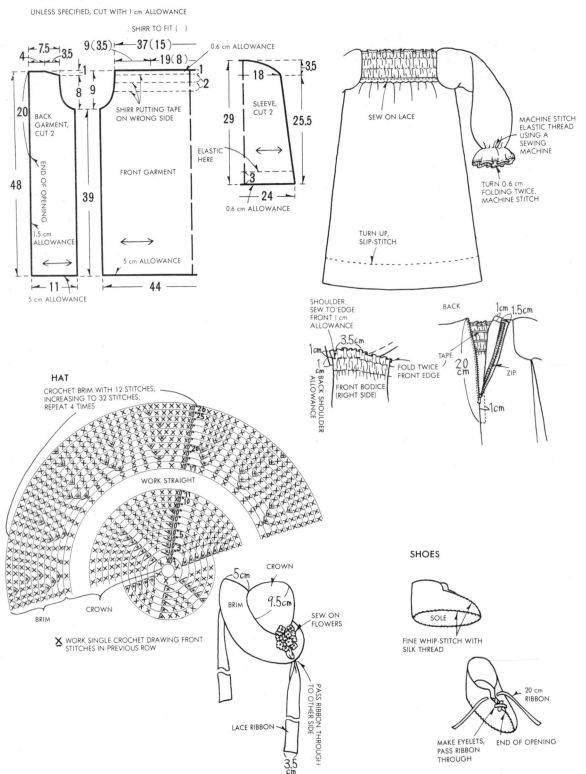

..SHIRR TO FIT ( )

9 (3.5) — 37 (15) —
4 — 7.5 — 3.5
19 (8)
0.6 cm ALLOWANCE

BACK GARMENT, CUT 2

20

48

END OF OPENING

1.5 cm ALLOWANCE

11

5 cm ALLOWANCE

SHIRR PUTTING TAPE ON WRONG SIDE

FRONT GARMENT

39

5 cm ALLOWANCE

44

ELASTIC HERE

18

SLEEVE, CUT 2

29

25.5

3.5

3

24

0.6 cm ALLOWANCE

SEW ON LACE

MACHINE STITCH ELASTIC THREAD USING A SEWING MACHINE

TURN 0.6 cm FOLDING TWICE, MACHINE STITCH

TURN UP, SLIP-STITCH

SHOULDER, SEW TO EDGE FRONT 1 cm ALLOWANCE

3.5 cm

1 cm BACK SHOULDER ALLOWANCE

FRONT BODICE (RIGHT SIDE)

FOLD TWICE FRONT EDGE

BACK

1 cm 1.5 cm

TAPE

20 cm

ZIP

1 cm

HAT

CROCHET BRIM WITH 12 STITCHES, INCREASING TO 32 STITCHES, REPEAT 4 TIMES

WORK STRAIGHT

BRIM

CROWN

X WORK SINGLE CROCHET DRAWING FRONT STITCHES IN PREVIOUS ROW

CROWN

5cm

BRIM

9.5cm

SEW ON FLOWERS

PASS RIBBON THROUGH TO OTHER SIDE

LACE RIBBON

3.5 cm

SHOES

SOLE

FINE WHIP-STITCH WITH SILK THREAD

20 cm RIBBON

MAKE EYELETS, PASS RIBBON THROUGH

END OF OPENING